I0060701

HOW TO WIN IN BUSINESS

How to Win in Business

Lessons I already learned for you

By

Kathleen Murphy

Published by Kathleen Murphy

Copyright© 2015 Kathleen Murphy

All rights reserved. No part of this publication may be reproduced, stored in a retrieval system, or transmitted in any form or by any means, electronic or mechanical, including photocopying, recording without either the prior permission in writing from the publisher as expressly permitted by law, or under the terms agreed.

The author's moral rights have been asserted.
ISBN Number **978-0692452271**

Cover by Maureen Doyle Reeder

Contents

PART 1

Introduction

Seizing the opportunity

There is a tide in the affairs of men which, taken at the flood, leads on to fortune
Shakespeare, Julius Caesar

So, you've dreamed up a brilliant idea for a new product which will conquer the world. Let's call it a weebee. You've even made a few weebees, tried them out, compared them with what's on the market already, and talked about them with a few friends. Their responses have been enthusiastic. Your weebee is going to be hot. You're on your way to your first million.

But: three little things are keeping you awake at night—and so they should:

1 - How do I protect my weebee so others won't see it and rip it off?

2 - How do I manufacture it in commercially viable quantities?

3 - How do I get people to buy it?

This book will put your mind at rest and start you on your way. The research has all been done for you, and I'm going to lay it out, one easy step after the other, right here.

From the outset, you need to keep several things in mind:

- Both the product and the business are your creations.
- You will succeed better if you have fun with them.
- Don't let them consume your life.
- Enjoy the process with your family.

Never forget that there are other things in your life that are even more important than your weebee, but at the same time, this once-in-a-lifetime venture could just be the most important thing you've ever done outside home and family. Done right, who knows where it might lead? With your will and determination and my notes and experiences, we can get it done right and keep a balance on both.

This book reflects that I'm a down-to-earth sort of person, and when I have personal experiences to pass on to help inspire you or show you the way, you can bet you'll hear them. So, expect to have some fun as we begin this journey together.

Here are a few highlights of what you need to do:

Protect your product

Do you want to hear a story of someone who made it big with her product and then lost it all? Well, read all about it in Part 2, and then, in Part 3, follow step-by-step guidelines on how to avoid my mistakes. You will learn how to protect your product from those would-be product vultures and gain some peace of mind. It doesn't take long to do and will only cost you a minimal fee[1] for initial patent pending protection. Once you've done it, you can breathe easy and get on with the more important things.

Through my experiences, you will be able to walk through the provisional patent application process. When you drop the news to people you want to do business with that your product already has a patent pending, they will see you as a professional from the outset.

Going to market

After we've talked about protecting your product, I will suggest a number of possible ways for you to market it. That will depend on what it is, of course. A new tank for the military would need a different strategy, and route, from boxes of pine cone-shaped scented soap. A kiosk in the mall could work for the soap but it won't shift too many tanks from your warehouse.

Learn from experience – mine!

More than anything, I want to show you exactly how to pursue your dreams. This book is based on my real-life experiences in business. It will show you, with lots of real-life examples, how I took my own first steps towards success and how I later followed up in order to develop and maintain the business.

---

[1] Filing fee correct as of March 2015: $260 ($130 for small entity, $65 for micro entity). I filed as a small entity, which is a small business.

What's that I hear you say? It sounds good but you're not a business person and you hate selling? I see, you're more of an ideas guy/gal. This book will help change your mind. I'm going to give you the inspiration to bring your product to market and I'm going to provide you with great ideas on how to market and patent and/or trademark your product.

Typically, half the fear of beginning a new project comes from not knowing how to go about it. On every page of this book you'll learn something that will help wash that fear away. No fear can conquer the will to begin, and the will to begin, coupled with the right know-how, adds up to success.

Whether you're introducing a new product or selling an existing one, the approach I am going to show you is a great way to take those first steps toward success. Who knows, this could be the start of a whole string of kiosks in malls all across the country selling your products—your patent-protected, well-produced, highly-sought-after products!

My experiences include developing products, from the initial inception of an idea through concept development to marketing. Although the kiosk approach to marketing has been an important part of my plan for one of my products, it is just one of the ways I have introduced my products to the world. You will learn about the others as well.

With faith and persistence, nothing can stop you. I'm a poor loser and there is nothing in my plan about losing YOU as a successful student and colleague.

We learn from our successes and I've had lots of those. We also learn from our failures, and I've had my share of those too. In these pages you will learn from both. There's no need for you to learn from your own failures when you can learn from mine.

The patent process – peace of mind for $130 (small entity)

It's important to start by getting the basics of the patent and trademark processes right. In Part 3, I'm going to show you how you can get a patent pending for just $130—a small price to pay for worry-free sleep. It will buy you a full year in which to determine whether or not your product has enough promise for you to go further with it.

It started with a kiosk

Some years ago during a major holiday season, I was asked to partner with someone who had an existing product. My job was to work at the kiosk each day while my partner took care of the details and bore the costs of the products and kiosk rent.

As it turned out, it was a great experience for me. I learned how to run a kiosk business and began to see wonderful possibilities for myself. Once I saw how successful we were, I was determined to start my own kiosk business and introduce my own products to that ready army of buyers that attack the malls every single day. The buyers are already there, brought there by the advertising of the big stores, but before they can get to those stores they have to come through you and your fascinating cart.

Back at the beginning, I was hesitant and afraid to start my own kiosk business. As a mother of three small children, finances were tight. At first, any outlay seemed too much upfront money. I needed to pay for the kiosk, pay for help, purchase the supplies, etc. Every time I turned around it seemed to cost me. What if the product didn't sell? What if I couldn't make the lease payments? All of those thoughts regularly romped through my mind.

The time came to have a talk with myself. "If you don't take the first step, you'll just continue to head nowhere fast," I said. "The worst that could happen is that you don't sell your products and you have to close down the kiosk. But at least you'll have tried."

I took steps to minimize any possible loss. I took out only a short-term lease on the kiosk. I stocked a minimum amount of product, but arranged to have easy access to more if needed. I worked it by myself as much as possible to avoid paying wages to others.

I was determined not to let fear stop me. I accepted that there was some risk but I believed in my product, and those with who I had talked about it, did too.

I had fears and I handled them by taking action. I secured a patent pending to deal with my fear of losing my product to a copycat. I made a reasonable arrangement with my manufacturer so I wouldn't worry about access to stock. I handled my fears by covering myself in every sensible way possible. Then, I stood myself up, took a deep breath and took a chance.

And guess what—I found that running the kiosk was easy!

Going through this book, based on my experiences, you will learn the basic steps that I took and those you

6

will take in starting a kiosk-based business, if this suits your product. You will be able to follow my progress from back when I started with my first one and up to my latest multi-mall kiosk venture. Most of my hints can be customized for you to use no matter what avenue you decide to use to market your product.

Learn from my success

Let me assure you, right from the start, that I have been very successful. I have worked with kiosks both on short and long term lease periods, and with patented, unique products in cooperation with manufacturers, so I know what is involved in making a success. The most basic thing I learned was that to succeed, a person has to have the *will* to succeed. Put past failures behind you. Don't dwell on the setbacks you have experienced. Never let yourself play the 'what if?' game. Learn from me and my business model and begin building your success from this moment forward.

Today is a new day. Fill it with new, essential information. Tailor it to your product and situation and *believe that you will succeed*. No matter what you have gone through in the past, no matter how many setbacks you may have had, today is a new day.

In the beginning I didn't have much start-up money or time. I worked at another job full time, was married, had a ton of bills, a home to run, and three young children who seemed to produce new bills every day. With my solid plan in place, having the faith and persistence to succeed was the only other thing I needed. Nothing would stop me.

Believe me, if I was able to do it, so can you!

PART 2

My Story: A Business Breakthrough

If you can imagine it, you can achieve it. If you can dream it, you can become it
William Arthur Ward

Remember how it was way back in 1989? Offices were filled with typewriters, large cumbersome phones that took up valuable space on the desk and great big Xerox copiers, with just a few large, square, tan-colored computers and printers sprinkled here and there. George Bush became president, the Berlin Wall fell, the San Francisco earthquake shook the Bay area, Lucille Ball died, and I made one of the most important decisions of my life. I remember it all so well.

I got up that morning, got my family organized and off for the day, and arrived at work with only minutes to spare. For me, it was another tedious day at work, during which I had to produce 1000 letters and 1000 matching envelopes. Day after day, month after month, I had the same tiresome task of preparing envelopes for 1000 letters. The printer was constantly jamming up and causing a mess. I would end up typing each envelope manually, as it wasn't worth the hassle of troubleshooting that early computer equipment. Work was not a happy place. It was filled with tedium and frustration and an all-too-scary sense of being trapped.

In 1989, typewriters were still king in the office. They were mostly used for typing envelopes, even stacks of 1000 at a time. The alternative method was to print labels and peel and stick one to each envelope—provided the sheet of labels didn't misfeed and give you half of each address on one label and half on the other.

One of the advances the computer brought was that you could print addresses directly on the envelope one at a time by manually inserting the envelope into the printer and hope it wouldn't jam or the glue wouldn't get too hot and stick either to the machine or the other envelopes. All of those alternatives only promised uncertain outcomes and were totally annoying. There had to be a better way!

My first big idea

Then that light bulb you see in comic strips lit up above my head—dimly at first, then brighter and brighter. What if there was an envelope already attached to a piece of paper, so that when you printed the letter, an envelope would print right along with it? Everything would print in one easy step. Everything would stay together and not be separated or have to be matched up later. The thought of the time and effort that would be saved was exhilarating.

Fortunately, my head wouldn't let things stop with just that thought and an idea was born. I was determined to create that very piece of stationery no matter what it took. My vision of how it would look was clear. I had a product just waiting to burst onto the scene.

Full instructions of what to do about a patent are in Part 3 so if you want to skip ahead then go for it. For those interested in what happens in real life, read ahead.

10

The first thing I did was research the patent industry to learn how to protect my product. Then I drew up a sketch of the letterhead/envelope combination (see Appendix VII) I put it into an envelope and mailed it to myself as proof of the date of inception. To date, I still have that unopened envelope in a safe place. I never want to give it up.

The next thing I did was fill out a disclosure document issued by the United States Patent and Trademark Office (USPTO) at uspto.gov. I went to my local library to obtain this basic information (it was before the days of Google). I filled out the disclosure document and sent it off certified mail to the patent office. (The disclosure program does not exist anymore, since you now have the option of a provisional patent.)

There were several questions for me to answer at the outset. What industry would produce and sell my product? How would I create the actual prototype? Were there any similar products already on the market? How could I determine if people in the work place thought it was a good idea? Who would buy it?

In 1989, we didn't have the information resources we have today, so I relied on the public library which was an excellent resource for me at the time. Every day after work and on Saturdays I could be found researching the United States Patent Office database. This database is updated on a regular basis so the information could be considered accurate.

I searched through the long files of current patents to see if my proposed product or any similar one existed. Once I felt confident that no similar product was already out there, I moved forward with my venture. I hired a patent attorney to perform a formal patent search. As suggested by my own research, he was unable to turn up anything similar either.

The crooked patent companies

Next, I needed to determine the proper way to patent the product (see Part 3). I came across the names of several invention submission companies that looked very promising. They talked a good game and made it sound as if they would help me get my product from where it was all the way to market. They also promised to secure a patent in my name.

Regrettably, I took a chance with one of them, only to find that its claims were misleading and its promises for a patent were false. The promise was for a 'design patent,' which, although relatively inexpensive and easy to obtain, would be worthless for my type of product. The company failed to mention that to me.

After several expensive false starts, I found that what I needed was called a 'utility patent.' This is the strongest patent, and will protect your product in a court of law should that ever become necessary. I discuss the different types of patents later on.

The invention companies—at least those I found— preyed on people with little or no knowledge of the patent industry. They took my money and in the end gave me nothing of any real value in return. That was a terrible disappointment after all the hope they had instilled in me.

HINT: If you are going to pay someone, pay a real patent attorney. You can usually arrange to pay such an attorney in stages as they compile the work.

The invention company also promised to help me find manufacturers for my product. They presented my product idea to a list of manufacturers who signed a non-use disclosure agreement. Later I discovered that a certain number of the manufacturers on the list had parent companies that weren't on the list, and parent companies were not bound by the non-use disclosure agreements of member companies. Several of the listed companies passed the information about my product on to their parent company.

That's where I hit disaster. That parent company, plain and simple, stole my product. I only found this out later.

Once I realized the fraudulent intentions of the invention company, I went back to my patent attorney. I was able to make payments to him as he progressed from step to step. I also talked my product up whenever the opportunity arose and eventually I found several serious investors along the way.

Patent attorney or DIY?

Before you hire anyone, do some investigating on your own. You have the world at your fingertips, as well as the vast public resources of the United States Patent Office (uspto.gov). Today, you don't actually have to hire an attorney. As I said, you can file your own patent and get a patent pending protection for just $130.00 for small entity. I have included the Provisional Application process in this book, see Part 3, 'Provisional Application for Patent,' which will give you basic steps in filing. I suggest, however, that at least for your first patent, consider hiring an attorney if you can afford one. They are the most knowledgeable in the area and already know the intricacies of the system—and you don't want to miss a step. Make certain you pick a *patent* attorney, since most attorneys have no idea how to go about the process.

I recommend that you file a provisional patent application as soon as you have an idea, because the new law states that the first person to file owns the invention, even if they didn't think of the idea first. There are certain things you need to be aware of when filing this application. They are outlined in this book as well as in material you can find at uspto.gov.

As I mentioned, there are different types of patents and the one that will best fit your product will depend on the type of product you are developing (see Part 3).

The best place to start researching the patent industry is the uspto.gov website. Be sure you get to the correct site, as there are many lookalike sites that try to mimic their site, hoping to sell you their products.

HINT: The provisional patent application is the easiest and the most affordable way to start the process.

If you start with the provisional application, you will have one year from the date you file the application during which you can test the market to see if your product does well and if it's worth moving forward from there. Once the application is filed, you are allowed to mark your product 'patent pending' as a warning to others to keep their hands off what you have. If, during that period, you get the feeling that it can be successfully marketed, you can continue with the patent process by filing for a *utility patent*. Let me state it one more time: *The utility patent is the best patent you can get to protect your product.*

It is extremely important that you include every possible scenario (use and form) in the *provisional patent application*, so when it comes time to file the *utility patent*, you won't have left anything out. The provisional patent application is the start of the application for Utility Patent.

You won't be able to add anything when it comes to completing the utility patent application, as it is merely an extension of the provisional patent application. In essence, it makes the original paperwork permanent. It is necessary to keep up to date on changes in the current patent laws at uspto.gov. This book is up to date as of the time it is being written, but laws change. Learn what is here first, then look at the USPTO.gov website. It will even direct you to recent updates and changes.

Once you get your *patent pending*, you can start test marketing and selling your product. Not knowing this back then, I waited until my patent was issued, ten years later, before I began marketing. This new opportunity for a provisional application provides an awesome advantage both in terms of time and expense!

Lessons learned (1)
• If you are going to pay someone, pay a real patent attorney. You can usually arrange to pay such an attorney in stages as they compile the work.

- I suggest that at least for your first patent, consider hiring an attorney if you can afford one.
- File a provisional patent application as soon as you have an idea, because the new law states that the first person to file owns the invention, even if they didn't think of it first.
- The provisional patent application is the easiest and the most affordable way to start the process.
- The utility patent is the best patent you can get to protect your product.

Going into production

Because of the type of product I had developed, I began approaching the office supply industry. Beyond that, I had no idea where to start. After extensive research, I discovered that my invention fell under the 'forms' industry category and my product was classified as a 'direct mail piece.' I actually invented the direct mailer. The envelope attached to the paper was folded over and mailed to a recipient who in turn filled out a form and used the envelope as a return envelope. The mailer was used in magazines for order forms, etc. Interestingly, this product was never used in the way I had originally intended for it to be used in business offices.

HINT: Don't limit the possible potential uses for any product.

What made my mailer a hot item was that it was compatible with laser printers and there was no competition. Many even thought that the problems creating a glue that was compatible with laser printers could not be overcome.

A sticky problem

At that time, form manufacturers were not typically set up to produce such a product from a mechanical standpoint. The envelope needed to be perforated where it met the paper, and the glue had to be compatible with laser printers, which produce a good deal of heat. Such heat tends to make traditional glues sticky. None of the manufacturers that could produce the form were familiar with any type of glue that was compatible with laser printers. This posed a major challenge in creating the product, but in the end gave me a tremendous advantage.

I now had to research the glue industry, another industry which with I was totally unfamiliar. After months of research and hundreds of calls and letters reaching out to glue manufacturers, I found one who had compatible glue that would work with my product. He sent me a letter with the glue specifications. I then brought the specifications to the manufacturer. We ended up using that glue and had another big success.

HINT: Just because you seem to hit a stone wall, don't give up.

I spent a good deal of time contacting possible distributors and eventually lined up close to four dozen of them who were interested in marketing the product to their clients. They committed to purchasing my product once it hit the market and I got it in writing. I had all of them sign non-disclosure documents prior to showing them the idea. These commitments helped eventually in getting the financing I needed to continue development and marketing.

I continued to have discussions with possible manufacturers and found several that were really interested in producing my product. It was so exciting to finally find someone willing to come on board.

The first company was located in Miami, Florida. They said they had the equipment necessary to produce the product so I traveled down to Miami to view the plant. They showed me the equipment they would use, but they still didn't have the glue. That was not my main concern at that point. I was thinking about using another method of sealing the envelope such as a label, but that would only defeat the purpose by adding an additional step for the user.

I went ahead and ordered several hundred pieces without the glue so I would have a prototype to use in my initial promotions. Once I had the prototype in one hand and a source for glue in the other, I took my product to several other companies that appeared to be equipped to manufacture the product.

There were many setbacks before I got to this point but nothing stopped me. Where there is a will there's a way. No matter what negativity I heard, I still pushed on, knowing I would eventually get this product to market.

I've already mentioned that many form distributor companies were interested in purchasing my products. One invited me to their office so I could show them what I had. Once I was there, they pulled out a beautiful package of products that were a duplicate of mine. A huge company had just come out with the same product!

My heart fell to my stomach. I could have given up at that point, but I didn't. I contacted them and got a copy of their patent and found out it had been issued after mine! I soon found that the firm was the parent of one of the companies on the list of the invention submission companies. The information had been given to a company months before, and they in turn created the product through their parent company. I documented everything from day one.

Meanwhile, I had a manufacturer who was interested in my product. I met with them and after a couple of hours of introducing the product and going through my presentation, they offered me a contract. This was so cool! You have no idea how I felt.

I got a license agreement from them to produce my product and they agreed to give me 20% on the gross sales. Unfortunately, once they found out about the company which was already producing the product and realizing the potential risk, they pulled out of our agreement. It was another sad setback.

I didn't give up. I went to my attorney, who wrote a 'cease and desist' letter to the infringing company. After weeks of arguing the patent claims back and forth for a while, they stopped making the product. I had an attorney do a case study and comparison of the patents to show the differences in our patents. I used the case study to continue my quest in finding a manufacturer. This also served as proof that my patent superseded their patent.

I had come to find out that the infringing company was on the verge of hitting the shelves of Office Depot. We were successful in stopping them from producing the product—or at least, I thought we were until sometime later. It turned out that another company stepped up with a patent that superseded both their patent and mine. They were actually the ones to stop the company from manufacturing the product, not me. That would have been a little too easy, for a small entrepreneur like me to be able to stop a Fortune 500 company.

I found out who the new company was and contacted them to see if there was something I could do to continue with my venture. I discovered that the patent they owned had never been used. They had obtained it so they could prevent other people from making the product. The company was the number one label marketing company in the country, if not the world, and they didn't want a product that would compete with theirs, especially on the shelves of office supply stores sitting right next to their product.

I was able to obtain a copy of their patent. I examined it and contacted its original owner. After we told him our story and how much time and money we had put into developing the product, he put me in touch with his attorney to see if something could be worked out. They ended up giving me a non-exclusive agreement to produce the product, with the promise of not putting it on the shelves of office supply stores (non-exclusive meant I was not the only one who could produce it). The product could not be sold as generic—it had to be personalized with specific customer information. That stipulation worked for me since I had planned on using manufacturers who sold through distributors and they usually sold forms as personalized anyway.

They could have dashed my dream right then and there but they felt for me as a small entrepreneur and gave me a chance. The same agreement they gave me for just a few thousand dollars they made available to other manufacturers at a cost of $500,000 plus a percentage of the product. Those larger companies didn't like the idea of having to sell the product in personalized form. They wanted to put a 'one-format-fits-all' version on the shelves of office supply stores. Although this was a limit, it gave me some breathing room.

I once again had a product to market. Woohoo! It would have been so easy just to give up. After all my work, I was determined to see the product hit the market, so I didn't even care if it had to be personalized. In fact, I would find ways to make that my advantage.

HINT: Don't give in to potential roadblocks until you have examined them from all possible angles.

At that point my adventure was up and running once again. I focused on finding a manufacturer to produce the product. At the time, I was only looking for one manufacturer. Had I known then what I know now, I would still be in the business. I would have seen that I had perhaps as many as ten manufacturers producing the product.

HINT: Be sure not to trap yourself into using just one manufacturer.

Manufacturers like to be in the driver's seat. You must not let them bully you. When you have several others to fall back on, you are in the driver's seat, and they understand that they really are working for you at your pleasure. Also, with several manufacturers working for you, if one should pull out, you have others to fall back on. In my case, however, I began by making one manufacturer very successful through creating my product

Striking a deal at last

Meanwhile, there were several other companies that were interested in producing my product. One in particular was a company located in Kansas. I liked them. The firm was presented to me as a family-owned business, and they seemed very trustworthy. Here starts an adventure which seems like a dream come true.

They flew my husband and me to Kansas City. It was winter and we drove through sleet and snow in our rental car for several hours before reaching our destination. Between the weather and the winding roads it was a good thing I wasn't driving or we might never have gotten there at all.

The company was housed in a large building. Inside, we were approached by a receptionist who showed us where we could wait until our contact person was ready to see us. He finally appeared and escorted us into a large conference room. The operation oozed class and know-how.

We took seats at a large table. A few minutes later several well-dressed men in coats and ties joined us. A young man called Kevin handed us an itinerary for the day, and we couldn't help but be impressed with the preparations that had been made on our behalf.

We were in our thirties, and I was the entrepreneur with a husband by my side. To them we were two New York-born-and-bred young people just starting out in this business.

The CEO of the company was also fairly young. We found out he was actually one of the partners and the son of the original owner.

A short, stocky man took control of the meeting with a brief introduction. We all then introduced ourselves. We were treated very professionally, and I had a feeling they knew what they wanted before we got there. It was a well-orchestrated meeting.

I must admit that by that point in the marketing process I had grown impatient. I wanted things to move along rapidly and get to the bottom line as soon as possible. I needed something to happen that day and was determined to leave with an agreement—"Do or die," I told myself.

The CEO started with some background, telling us that they were a business that thrived on new products and were known as an innovator of new forms. They had been in business for over forty years and were very family oriented.

The nature of my product was presented, after which the CEO asked each of his people for their opinion about it. All their comments were very positive. It was reassuring to me that they understood its true potential. So many other people I'd met had tried to point out the possible negative aspects of my idea—probably to soften me up so I would be happy to receive less than my product deserved.

HINT: Be sure to stay away from negative people and people who don't want you to succeed.

The CEO then showed us a form that was similar to mine in many ways. It was printed on less sturdy paper and was clearly not compatible with a laser printer. He asked me for my opinion as to why someone would want to use my product instead of that one. I took their form and held it in my hand for a minute. Then I picked up my form and held it in my hand for a minute. Their form was made of a flimsy piece of paper with a so-called 'envelope' attached, which was oddly small. Its quality was very poor. My form was thick. It was your typical 8.5" by 11" letterhead, attached to a real 8.5" envelope. And mine had been developed specifically to be compatible with laser printers. I knew the market, I knew my product and could see they were very different.

Something came over me and I had the urge to be forthright even though I felt that it would be unprofessional surrounded by all these executives. I decided to go with my gut. I threw their form on the table and began.

"This is a piece of crap. Look. When you open it, the entire piece falls apart. Plus, it is no way compatible with laser printers. It would come apart in the process. Printers would be constantly jammed and the employees would be constantly frustrated."

They had clearly not been prepared for that. They remained silent for a long moment. Finally, one of them responded.

"Kathleen, you are absolutely right," he said. "This is a piece of crap. There is no comparison between it and yours." He was backed by a chorus of nods around the table.

I was finally off and running down the road toward success. An agreement was drawn up and the terms were discussed. We had to make sure the items were personalized to each of the end users. We agreed on percentages of the gross profit, so much for the label company and so much for me. My earnings would be paid monthly. Other stipulations to our agreement, which was never signed, included the right to audit their books, and the requirement that I sign off on every project.

In some ways it had been a surreal series of events. It was one of those 'pinch me to make sure it's really happening' times in my life. Let me tell you, it really was happening.

At the conclusion of the meeting they showed us around the plant. They showed us their existing equipment. They took us through the manufacturing process of each piece. It was pretty cool. The plant was similar to the Miami location I had visited, but it was a much larger operation. As it turned out, Miami was actually too hot to produce my product. The plant couldn't keep the glue cool enough to work with. Now that was something I hadn't thought about.

After all was said and done, they needed to purchase some new equipment to make my product. It was an extension to an existing piece they already had. The cost would come to nearly a million dollars, so to spend that kind of money they were clearly dedicated.

That night we checked into a bed and breakfast. It was a house that had been built in the 1800s and was Victorian in style. It was amazing—large, showy, and beautifully appointed. I will always remember the staircase. It seemed to go on forever. The accommodation was two-room suites—bedroom and sitting room. It made for a much-needed evening of relaxation. Needless to say, things like that were not a usual part of our life.

When we first entered the room, my eyes were immediately directed to a colorful welcome package from the company. It was arranged perfectly. There was a postcard of the hotel, a picture of the small town, a bottle of wine, cookies, and other thoughtful items. It was really neat.

We couldn't help but be swayed a bit by their behavior, but sometimes things aren't as good as they appear to be. We discovered that the agreement was not everything it should have been. It had been a handshake deal with nothing put in writing. It was a partnership agreement based on trust. Unfortunately, there often seems to be no place for trust in business. I learned several valuable lessons, however, and I can now pass them on to you.

My two biggest mistakes were having a written agreement that wasn't signed, and giving them an exclusive arrangement. Even though my agreement with the patent owner wasn't exclusive, they said ours would have to be or they were not going to produce the product.

Dumb! I had other manufacturers who could have produced the product as well.

But it wasn't all bad news. The product was soon introduced to over 500 distributors. This included the distributors I had been working with. My product was introduced as a mailer which was pre-printed and personalized for the companies that placed their orders through the distributors. My checks ranged from $1,500 to about $3,000 each month during the first year.

During that first year I kept very involved with the company as far as marketing the product was concerned. I was in direct contact with the product manager on a regular basis. During that process, I got an SBA business loan to use in marketing the product on a larger scale.

HINT: Always draw up a business plan.

With the completion of my business plan I had everything in place to get approved for the loan.

Lessons learned (2)
- Don't limit the possible potential uses for any product.
- Just because you seem to hit a stone wall, don't give up.
- Don't give in to potential roadblocks until you have examined them from all possible angles.
- Be sure not to trap yourself into using just one manufacturer.
- Stay away from negative people and people who don't want you to succeed.
- Always draw up a business plan.

Another missed opportunity

While working with the company, I also presented an idea for a label/letter combo mailer and was told it was already out there. Guess what—it wasn't. That would have been the one. They are still producing these types of products. The patents on each one were filed well after that time. If only I had filed when I thought of the idea, I would have had the rights for production and marketing.

Another idea I had was to create a piece of software that would be compatible with my product and make it much easier to use. The manufacturer found a software company to create a template based on my idea. I assisted them with the project, making sure it was done correctly. It had been another mistake. I should have insisted on an additional royalty on that, too. They just did things as if they were doing it as a favor to me.

We also used a trademark that I designed. The trademark process was a little pricey as I had an attorney research it for me and he kept coming back with, "It's already taken." Even so, I did some research of my own on the USPTO data base. I located the company that owned the trademark I wanted. I contacted them via mail and they responded. They allowed me to have the name. So, hundreds of dollars later, I got the name I wanted with really no help from my attorney. Go to the uspto.gov website and click on Trademarks, then do a search through the TESS system.

HINT: First, go ahead and do your own research. Then, if you feel you need additional professional help, you can obtain it.

I allowed the forms company which was making my product to use my trademark name for it. Later, I discovered that I should have charged them for its use. It's not easy to come up with a name that fits a product perfectly, and the perfect name really boosts sales.

We worked on marketing pieces using my written material and photos which described and promoted the product. We created a website to introduce it to the public. In addition to those methods, I also marketed the product through ,industry trade shows and stationery shows and through direct sale at a kiosk. I was very successful in all these areas.

The end of the honeymoon

We were thrilled with our new relationship with our manufacturing hero but it didn't last. After about a year, the company contacted me saying they didn't want me involved in the operating phase any more. They advised me to be content just sitting back and collecting a check each month. In fact, if I didn't follow that plan they threatened to stop producing the product. I figured it would actually be an easy way to continue making a good deal of money while ridding myself of a lot of work and stress, so I accepted the offer.

Hint: Don't ever step back. If I hadn't stepped back, they couldn't have let me go because I would have been considered a solid partner in the development of the form.

I had been receiving around $5,000 a month for nearly five years when out of the blue I got a letter from their new attorney, who was not familiar with the history of the product, indicating that he had determined the product was not mine and that because of that I shouldn't have been getting any money from it all those years. I proceeded to document everything we had been through but in the end they went to the label company directly and received a license from them. That effectively bypassed me.

So, after all the years I had worked with the company to make the product a success, they dropped me like a hot potato. It was more than a little disappointing.

I contacted the label company and they said that since it had been a non-exclusive arrangement with me, they had every right to give them a separate agreement but said I could also continue to produce the product under my original agreement. Since I had been out of the picture for four years, thanks to the manufacturer's threat, I no longer had any customers to sell it to. They had absorbed all my customers when they demanded that I stand down and perhaps this was their intention all along.

I made several mistakes that you will NOT make. I had been so concerned about getting the product to market that I didn't think about keeping it on the market once it got there. If I hadn't listened to the Kansas company and gone with them as non- exclusive, I could have had multiple manufactures making the product and maybe instead of $5,000 a month I would have been receiving $50,000 a month.

That is why it is so important to set yourself up correctly. Don't give up any rights without having everything spelled out in writing. A partnership agreement means you are partners and will continue for as long as the product continues. Make sure that is how you set things up. Have an attorney draft an agreement for you and make sure it is signed by both parties.

HINT: Stay involved in the marketing of your product.

As the years went by, that situation continued to just eat me up. I had a list of all of our clients from day one. Since those clients had been mine, I knew them on a personal level.

At first I tried to win them over, but I didn't have another manufacturer in place to back me. I thought that at least I should warn other entrepreneurs not to go with the company that had treated me so badly. I had come to find out that they were not the folksy, family-owned business they pretended to be. They were not trustworthy. In essence, they had stolen my ideas and my products, and once they were in control and my products were in demand, they eased me out.

I sought out my original contact at the business, and told him my intentions. I was going to contact each of my clients to let them know what had happened. I had kept the letters and full documentation of the way they had cheated me out of my business. He asked to see the list of clients, not believing, I am sure, that I had really kept it. He was pretty amazed that I had every one of his major clients listed, along with the contact person for each one.

In the end, they made me an offer that appeared to be the best I would be able to get. What they had done was unethical and immoral, but not strictly illegal. I found myself in that familiar situation of something being better than nothing. Part of the agreement was that I agreed not to use their name in a book I was writing.

I settled and took the money. If I had taken them to court, it would have cost a six-figure sum in legal fees, and who knows if I would have won. Even if there was a good chance of winning, I was tired of the fight and would not have wanted to continue a relationship with that sort of company anyway.

The company is located in Kansas. I'm not allowed to say much more but I sincerely doubt if I need to. Please beware.

Sometimes when you're a little guy with no money and you have a great idea, a big guy will come along and wine and dine you and then take advantage of you— sometimes, it appears, by outright bullying. "Do what I say, or I'll stop making your product. Don't try to use other manufacturers as it may mean no one will market or produce your product."

I wish I had known what a hot product it actually was. I would never have stepped back and I most certainly would have had more than one company making it. Had I done that, even if they had all gone to the label company five years later, I at least would have made a small fortune.

Now that I think about it, there were many ways I could have threatened them. Making the product on their own for all those years without my involvement would have been a direct violation of a patent they didn't have the rights to. They didn't have me sign off on projects the way I was supposed to. And who knows, maybe they weren't putting the proper percentage aside for the label company and maybe I was making much less than I was due. I had not taken advantage of the part of our non-signed agreement that said I had the right to audit their books.

Hindsight is 20/20. And because of that I am now able to help others learn the ropes, so they can become successful.

Lessons learned (3)
- File the idea with the patent office when you think of it.
- Insist on additional royalties when your product is used.
- Do your own research on trademarks.
- Charge anyone that uses your trademark.
- Don't ever step back.
- Don't give up any rights without having everything spelled out in writing.
- Stay involved in the marketing of your product.

PART 3

The lessons I learned

All our dreams can come true, if we have the courage to
pursue them
Walt Disney

Using a mentor or a coach

As I said before, if I had known then what I know now, I would have done things very differently. I took too many WRONG steps and lost a lot. Let me set out the RIGHT steps so you can learn from my experience and benefit.

Using a mentor is one of the right steps. In fact, this may be the ultimate tool. Mentors are people who already know the ropes and can offer expert guidance. They can give you experience-based suggestions and support you as you find your starting place and help you to move forward.

Once you're ready to start a business, you'll have many important decisions to make. This is especially true during the initial planning stages and the first months of getting your business up and running. Ultimately, of course, you are responsible for your decisions, but when they are based on the knowledge and expertise of mentors who have already been there, you are miles ahead of trying to do it all by yourself. A mentor will be an invaluable resource to you. He or she can answer your questions, but more importantly, he or she can help you identify the right questions.

A mentor is someone who has achieved the goals towards which you are striving and who started from the same place you are in right now. They have already done the work to get there so know how to advise you and point you in the right direction, they have achieved their goals so are a great example of what is possible and most important. They are available to you so you can learn from their experience without them needing to gain anything personally. They are a support mechanism. I relied on my husband, who really didn't know much about what I was going through, but he was there to support my every move. This kept me going but didn't protect me from mistakes.

Finding a mentor

One of the biggest mistakes I made was not to use a mentor, but it was not until I lost all that I had gained that I learned how I could benefit from one. There are various free resources where you can find someone who is familiar with your industry, trade and/or products, to mentor you at no charge.

Government-sponsored organizations

There are various government-sponsored mentor organizations that I highly recommend and one in particular that I like is called SCORE, the Service Corps of Retired Executives. SCORE describe themselves as "a non-profit association dedicated to entrepreneur education and the formation, growth, and success of small businesses nationwide."

The SCORE network has more than 12,000 retired business executives, leaders, is sponsored by the SBA (Small Business Association), and has volunteers who share their expertise in person and online.

The SBA site also has information on the following services:

- Assistance to small businesses about issues such as finances, marketing, technical problems, production, among other things (<u>Small Business Development Centers</u>).
- For women, there is a special resource that provides training and counseling that supports and helps them grow successful businesses (<u>Women's Business Centers</u>).
- For minorities, the Minority Business Development Agency exists to provide information and support about exporting if you're interested in global business, contract opportunities, or if you require access to information about grants and loans, and anything to do with mergers, acquisitions plus joint ventures (<u>Minority Business Development Centers:</u> www.mbda.gov).

Trade associations

Trade associations represent the following: industries, certain sections of the population such as genders and ethnic groups, alongside business types. Their support can include mentoring programs so be sure to research your area carefully and see if you can identify any that may be useful to you in building your business. If you need help finding one that suits your needs consult any internet search engine or the SBA site (sba.gov).

Mentoring for government contractors

If your business plans to sell anything to the federal government, it can be tough to get started for various reasons to do with regulations and requirements. There is help available through a Mentor/Protégé Program offered by the General Services Administration (GSA). The program attempts to help small businesses gain government contracts and increase their performance when applying for them.

The few examples I have mentioned serve to show that if you look for it, you can find help with most business issues and within diverse industries.

Naming, incorporating, & registering your business

One of the most personal aspects to running a business is the name you provide. You may have chosen something that is important to you or something a bit random. If you want your name to be part of your brand and ensure that nobody else uses it, you need to do two things before you buy any marketing material, including business cards:

1.   Do a name search to make sure someone else isn't already using it for your kind of business.
2.   Get a trademark.

You can do both of these through the Trademark Office which is what I did. I first searched to find out if anyone else was using the name we had chosen and then got a trademark.

There are other ways to get a name for your business, however. You don't have to get a trademark unless you want to reserve the name for yourself and ensure no one else can use it nationally as well as locally.

There are different ways to register a company and each provides you with different considerations about legal, financial and tax considerations. You could set up as a sole proprietor of a company, a corporation or as a limited liability company.

Sole Proprietor

The easiest and quickest way to begin your organization is as the sole proprietor of your business. It's a cheaper way to do things at the beginning and you can change the structure of your company as it gets bigger.

Each state has its own rules so to avoid issues with variation, be sure to contact your local government, usually the county clerk's office, to find out what is required for naming your business. For example, even if you register with the state, you may still have to register for licensing purposes with the local government depending on your local authority.

The following are basic steps from my experience and what I have encountered. You may not have to register your name if you are using your last name in the name of your business. For any other registrations you can contact your county clerk's office, sometimes at the state level, as a DBA (Doing Business As) or as an assumed name or fictitious name.

LLC or corporation

You can set up an LLC or a corporation. You could do this yourself at your secretary of state website.

If you live in Florida, for example, you would do a Google search such as Florida SOS. You could usually register right online by filling out an application and including a filing fee. Each state varies. Be sure to register your business with your local authorities so you are licensed and permitted to do the type of work you are doing.

As I mentioned before, if you want to brand your name, I would recommend a trademark.

Filing for a tax ID number

You have to obtain a tax id number if you are going to register as a corporation or llc. You could use your social security number if you are filing as a sole proprietor. Go to irs.gov to get one. You could usually get the tax id number on the spot. It doesn't cost anything to obtain a tax id. Many companies will charge you to get it for you when you could do this on your own. It is very easy.

Sales Tax Number

You need a sales tax number in order to collect taxes for your products. You can obtain one through your local government and you will have to file quarterly or monthly. The best way to deal with tax is to be prepared. Put a percentage of each sale aside as you carry on with your business. This will make life a lot easier. Contact your state to obtain a sales tax number. A google search will bring the information up for you.

Raising finance

As I mentioned earlier on, I obtained financing in a couple of different ways. I couldn't depend on my family, as they didn't even want to understand my product, never mind lend me any money. Plus, they probably didn't have the means to lend. Your best bet is friends and/or perhaps a small business loan. Today it is really tough to get the lending you need from banks. Back in the day, it was a lot easier. Today you have the opportunity to apply for grants through the government.

You could also look for funding through crowd funding. This is where people find interest in your product and want to donate money to help you bring it to market. You could do an internet search for more information.

You could also look at the Community Development Fund website (cdfi.gov). This is a fund into which financial institutions donate to help companies with lending. You have to review the site to see if it works for your needs.

You may also want to explore venture capitalists. I had a couple of close friends lend me some money and I was lucky enough to pay them back when the product started to make a profit. I was also lucky enough to find a bank to lend to me through the SBA. I used the money to create the prototype and for marketing at trade shows. The process of the SBA loan was tedious and I had to prepare an accurate business plan.

Your business plan

A business plan is an actual plan of the route your business will take as it grows. It will help you tremendously because it will make you think about your future and how you are going to succeed.

Everyone can benefit from a business plan since it will enable you to predict financial growth. It will have to be modified from time to time to fit your needs. I made a business plan and included all the necessary documents, including the commitments I received from my clients to buy. Remember earlier when I mentioned my research in finding distributors in the industry? Well, that paid off.

I would recommend doing an internet search for samples of existing business plans related to your field. You could follow the format using your own information. This will give you a great start in developing an organized business plan.

Protecting your product

Patents and trademarks

My history with losing a unique product I created makes this is my favorite part. How are you going to protect your product?

My first, and strongest, recommendation is for a patent. There are different patents available to apply for, depending on the type of product you have to offer. Today you have so many resources to do research right, you could hire an attorney, or you could file yourself. I would recommend an attorney or patent agent if you can afford it. Remember the **first to file** is the owner of the invention—it used to be first to invent.

Before I continue, I want to give you a basic explanation of what a patent is and the types of patents available to you. I want to focus on utility patents, design patents and the provisional patent application.

What is a patent?

According to the US Patent and Trademark Office, a patent is a property right granted by the government of the United States of America to an inventor "to exclude others from making, using, offering for sale, or selling the invention throughout the United States or importing the invention into the United States" for a limited time in exchange for public disclosure of the invention when the patent is granted.

Types of patents

Utility Patent

This is issued for the invention of a new and useful process, machine, manufacture, or composition of matter, or a new and useful improvement thereof. It generally permits its owner to exclude others from making, using, or selling the invention for a period of up to twenty years from the date of patent application filing, subject to the payment of maintenance fees. Approximately 90% of the patent documents issued by the USPTO in recent years have been utility patents, also referred to as "patents for invention."

Basic Filing Fee: $140 (Paper), $70 (Electronic filing) (Small Business Entity).

Design Patent

This is issued for a new, original, and ornamental design embodied in or applied to an article of manufacture. It permits its owner to exclude others from making, using, or selling the design for a period of fourteen years from the date of patent grant. Design patents are not subject to the payment of maintenance fees. Please note that the fourteen-year term of a design patent is subject to change in the near future.

Basic filing fee: $90.00 (Small Entity Fee).

Plant Patent

Issued for a new and distinct, invented, or discovered asexually reproduced plant, including cultivated sports, mutants, hybrids, and newly-found seedlings, other than a tuber-propagated plant or a plant found in an uncultivated state. It permits its owner to exclude others from making, using or selling the plant for a period of up to twenty years from the date of patent application filing. Plant patents are not subject to the payment of maintenance fees.

Basic filing fee: $90.00 (Small Entity Fee). (Source: www.uspto.gov/web/offices/ac/ido/oeip/taf/patdesc.htm)

Copyright

This protects a product that is a literary, dramatic, musical, or artistic work.

Trademark

A trademark is a word, phrase, symbol, and/or design that identifies and distinguishes the source of the goods of one party from those of others.

Application for Registration: $375.

Provisional Patent Application

A provisional patent application will prove the date of your invention, as it is used as an effective early filing date. You could also mark your product "patent pending" once it is filed. Like myself, you may come across someone with the same patent claiming they filed first. Your provisional patent application will prove the original filing date. I would recommend to file the provisional patent application as soon as possible. Remember the first to file owns the patent.

Basic Filing fee: $130 (Small Entity Fee).

Check website for the most up-to-date prices on filing fees.

The patent process

Please note that the basic filing fees refer to the initial filing fee. Check out the USPTO current fee schedule for more information.

I did everything myself in the beginning, including the initial patent search. Remember I had to go to a public library and pull out old disks and use antiquated computers that may or may not have been updated. It took hours, but I didn't care. I wanted to be sure before I moved forward with a patent application.

The patent process can be challenging if you are not familiar with it. I aim to give you enough information to enable you to at least understand the process.

A **utility patent** lists all the claims relating to your product. It is one of the strongest patents out there which will protect your product by listing the summary, claims, and drawings of every inch and the exact process on how it is so be as thorough as possible.

Patents become public information. That means anyone could get a copy of your patent, and make a change to the product and get a patent on the same invention. So you want to make sure you cover everything when writing your claims. If an attorney is doing it for you, be sure he or she is aware of every single scenario. And make sure it is part of the claim.

How to perform a patent search

The ways to perform a patent and/or a trademark search are as follows:

First, through the USPTO website. Type 'Patent Search' in the search field and it will bring you to the site to perform a search. In Patents, 'Quick Search' will allow you to search USPTO's comprehensive patent database by patent number or keywords.

- Enter the keywords you think would best fit your product.
- When a patent pops up that is similar to yours, you can open it, read the claims and look at the drawings to compare to your product.

Inside that patent will be a list of other patents that will also be similar to your product. These patents were the ones used to compare with the current patent you are looking at.

The attorney or patent agent had to fight for his/her patent by arguing specific claims in each patent to show why his/her patent is different. Typically, the first patent application you file is denied and you have to fight for the patent based on claims or prior art. This may take years. But at least this gives you a great insight and idea whether your product is already out there.

A thorough patent examination at the USPTO may uncover US and non-US patents as well as non-patent literature. You will also want to do an internet search to see if your product is out there and check any available media such as books, magazines, the internet, and uspto.gov.

Once you find that the product is not out there, then you can proceed in a direction that best fit your needs according to your type of patent.

A **design patent** is very easy to get but it gives virtually no protection. The utility patent, as mentioned earlier, is your strongest patent. Also, if you go for the utility patent you can start the process by filing the Provisional Patent application. This gives you one year to file for the utility patent, which is going to have to include the same claims as the provisional patent application, because you won't be able to change them when the time comes to file the utility patent. So you have to be very careful when preparing the application, as you want to be sure to include everything in it.

Provisional application for patent

To understand how important the provisional application for a patent is, you will need some background. As I already mentioned, filing a Provisional Application for Patent is one of the fastest and easiest ways to start protecting your invention. I suggest you read the information on the USPTO website at this URL: http://www.uspto.gov/patents-getting-started/patent-basics/types-patent-applications/provisional-application-patent

The provisional application for a patent provides you with twelve months of protection from the date you filed. This option has only been available since June 8, 1995. It is useful for all of us so make sure you take advantage of its availability. See www.uspto.gov for further or updated information.

There is some great information on the USPTO website about the differences between Trademarks, Patents, Copyright, and everything we have so far been discussing. The information is available as a video and as a printable transcript of the video that is provided as a Word document (see http://www.uspto.gov/trademarks-getting-started/trademark-basics).

How to file a provisional application

The provisional application papers (written description and drawings), filing fee, and cover sheet can be filed electronically at the USPTO website. Use the Search feature and type in 'Provisional Patent Application filing'. At the time of writing the URL was as follows: http://www.uspto.gov/patents-getting-started/patent-basics/types-patent-applications/provisional-application-patent

As USPTO say:

"A provisional application for patent (provisional application) is a U.S. national application filed in the USPTO under 35 U.S.C. §111(b). A provisional application is not required to have a formal patent claim or an oath or declaration. Provisional applications also should not include any information disclosure (prior art) statement since provisional applications are not examined. A provisional application provides the means to establish an early effective filing date in a later filed nonprovisional patent application filed under 35 U.S.C. §111(a). It also allows the term "Patent Pending" to be applied in connection with the description of the invention" (From: Provisional Application Patent—USPTO website).

Be sure to follow their directions exactly.

Trademark search

To perform a trademark search, go to the USPTO search field and type in 'Trademark Search.' This will bring you to the USPTO database. You can conduct a search online for free using the TESS (Trademark Electronic Search System) database.

As USTPO say:

"Trademarks are an essential part of your business. They represent your goodwill, your reputation, and they're how people can tell the difference between the products and services that your business offers and what other businesses offer."

Examples of usage are presented through global brands to explain what is meant by all the definitions and descriptions.

The following gives you a flavor for the kind of information available:

"Now, you probably recognize these as brands for soft drinks, right? We have Coca-Cola and Pepsi. Now, when you see each mark on a can or a bottle, you immediately know the source of the beverage. Now, you also know that it's not the competitor's beverage. See, it distinguishes them. That way, you don't drink a Coke when you want a Pepsi and vice versa.

Now, Coca-Cola is a trademark in itself, but as you can see here, it is also displayed in a distinctive script, and the display of the wording in that stylized form is also a mark.

Pepsi is also a word mark, but, as you can see here, it is also shown in a particular format, and the combination of the wording and the design, well, that's also a mark.

[...]

It could be a sound. Or a color. Or even a smell. Pretty much anything can be a trademark or service mark, so long as it identifies the source of goods and services and distinguishes them from the goods and services of others" (From: Basic Facts about Trademarks—USPTO website).

Marketing your product

Once you have a patent pending, you can start marketing your product. If you are looking for a manufacturer or a license agreement, be sure to have them sign a non-disclosure agreement, even if you have a patent pending. (A non-disclosure agreement states they will not pass on information about the product to others or use it themselves to produce, describe, or market the product.)

Be sure to include the marketing plan as part of your business plan. A market analysis to determine the pricing of your product(s) can be a huge help. Mine was a lot easier, since I had a manufacturer in place who provided me with that information. You may have to do a little more research.

A marketing plan lists all the ways you will put your efforts into practice in reference to marketing your product or products. It's a way of outlining in a coherent and concise method, all your strategies.

My business plan

Think of the business plan as telling someone all about your business, the market in which it will work, and how you are going to make money from it. Describe how and why your business will succeed while others around you have failed.

Templates for business plans are available for free online so don't think you have to create one from scratch. One resource for some simple plans is the Office Online site (https://templates.office.com).

I included the following information on my plan. You don't need to have all the information and in the same way that I added them. A business plan should be aimed at the information that is specific to you and formatted around the audience to who you will be pitching it. See the following for an example:

- A cover sheet
  o This included basic information to explain the contents and to who it belonged.
- An executive summary (statement of business purpose)
  o Your priority is to get the executive summary right because this is the part that most people will read first, and if you can't sell them on your idea here they might not read on. This is a chance to sell yourself. Be inspiring and be creative.
  o This section will consist of your key points and highlights.
- A table of contents
  o Provide clarity and consistency for your readers. Let them know where everything is located within your business plan. A table of contents is also a useful tool for you to quickly glance through and make sure you have everything that you need.
- A business description

- o Mention the purpose of your business and what you will be doing.
- Marketing on the competition
  - o You can include your marketing plan here or a reference to your marketing plan. You need to show that you understand the market in which you will be working and that you stand out from the rest.
  - o Be sure to show your awareness of any opportunities and threats to your business. This will require that you consider your strengths and weaknesses.
  - o Apply the same process to your competitors as well. Your plan needs to show that you have a clear strategy for dealing with them.
- Operating procedures
- Personnel and business insurance
  - o Provide sufficient detail on what type of insurance will cover your personnel and your business.
- Financial data [see Appendix IV]
  - o Your business plan's financial information will face particular scrutiny. Cash flow needs to be documented in full—there is further information about this further down in the business plan. Your sales predictions need to be evidence based and founded on reliable information. You will more than likely have better information about what your costs will be, but you need to be able to predict sales as well. Don't miss out on either of these. Ask for help if you need it. Ask people who have gone through similar processes. An accountant would have valuable advice and a mentor would be a great person to turn to as well. Turn to people who have the experience to guide you and be realistic.

- Loan applications
  o List the appropriate information from all the banks you have contacted and what the terms are of any loans you have taken out.
- Capital equipment and supply list
- Balance sheet
- Break-even analysis
- Profit and loss statements
- Three-year summary
- Detail by month, first year
- Detail by quarters, second and third year
- Assumptions upon which projections were based
- Pro forma cash flow
  o There are plenty of examples of profitable companies that have had to shut down because they had issues with their cash flow. Just because you can show that your business will be making a profit doesn't mean that you will have enough cash to make sure you are solvent and be able to pay your bills as they become due. You need to show that you have thought about how you will manage your business in a way that implements effective cash flow management measures.
- Supporting documents
- Tax returns of principals (my own since I was the only person in the business) for the last three years
- Personal financial statements (obtained from the bank)
- Copies of licenses and other legal documents (including a copy of my patent)
- Copies of resumes of all principals (myself and a potential manager with many years of experience)

- Copies of letters of intent from suppliers

A business plan is not a one-format answer to everything. Try and tailor the information you provide to your audience. A new retailer will want to see different things, so that they can work with you in confidence, than a bank who are interested in loaning you money. An investment trust looking to fund you might be more interested in your history and what kind of support you need, for example.

Do your homework about what each potential reader will want to know. Keep updating your business plan as it will be useful for you as well to see how your changes in business may require you to adjust your projections or your financial situation. Use your business plan to keep up with your market and yourself.

You will want to calculate your profits and could follow the formula below to give you an idea how to do this.

Calculating profit

Profit is the amount left over after your production costs. Non-production costs are subtracted from gross (total) revenue. Some of the cash-flow and profits must be put back into the business to sustain inventories, accounts receivable, capital equipment purchases, and other assets.

Case study on how I calculated profit:

I created and designed different products including a gel candle design. The gel candles were very new to the industry when I was creating my designs. They were a product for which I had to calculate the cost and profit and I did so in the following way: I would calculate the cost to make the product, then multiply it by two for wholesale and then double that total for retail price. If the product cost me $5 to make, I would charge $10 wholesale and $20 retail. This gave me room to play with the cost. That made it pretty easy for me to calculate. Now in today's market, I may go $15 for retail. You have to determine the profit margin that will fit your needs.

A formula for retail price

Here is a formula that might make it easier to visualize.

Production costs (labor + materials)

(+) Non-Production Costs (overhead + marketing + profit)

(=) Total Costs (all costs)

Total Costs x Markup Percentage = Retail Price

($10.00) x (1.50) = ($15.00) } markup 50%

Retail Price $15.00

(-) Total Costs $10.00

(=) Gross Margin Percentage $5.00 } gross margin 33%

Keeping track of your sales

I recommend you set up an accounting method to track your sales. You could use accounting software, an accountant, or just an accounting book. You will also want to set up a business bank account.

I always recommend getting at least two accounts, one for the operating costs and the other for sales and federal taxes. This way the money for taxes doesn't mix in with your operating expenses and you won't spend it. If you have to borrow from it, at least you know you have to put it back. To open a bank account you usually need the filing documents, either the state or county documents, along with two forms of identification. Be sure to find out the different ways to avoid maintenance fees before opening an account.

Where to market

Two great places to start selling your products are trade shows and kiosks. You can search for trade or gift shows and narrow down the locations to the ones closest to you. This is a great way to find opportunities to showcase your products.

Trade shows

As I mentioned earlier, trade shows were one of the places where I marketed my letter/envelope invention. Every year, the forms industry holds a huge trade show where all the distributors go to learn about new innovative products. One of the form magazines offered free membership to their magazine, where you could get a free listing. One year, they ran a forms contest and I ended up winning a Silver Award from the industry for my letter/envelope design. I was flown out to Reno, Nevada to accept the award.

More importantly, at the trade show, I gathered many leads. Follow up is the key to success in any type of show you attend. One of the ways I would gather the information is to promote a drawing for a specified amount of products. I would collect business cards throughout the show and at the end of the show, I would pull a name and give them the prize. This was a great way to get names without having to ask for their information up front for specific advertising.

Throughout the show, I would demonstrate my product using a computer, printer and folder. The distributors were in awe of the product. So be prepared to demonstrate to pique interest. Many of those leads became loyal clients.

Another method to market your product is with kiosks or carts which also allow you to test your product by introducing it to the end user. That's how I introduced my gel candle designs. If I had had professional packaging for my designs, gift shows would have been a great way to get the product on shelves of larger retail stores. Buyers of products attend gift shows. You have to be prepared to sell hundreds of items with a 'net 30-day.' That means you have to lay out the money for the product, make it and deliver it, and hope you get paid within 30 days. Usually you do, but it can take time. You'll need the funds and resources but it could prove to be very lucrative.

You may also want to approach 'Mom & Pop' stores to see if they could put your product up, maybe on consignment, or maybe they'll buy some from you at wholesale pricing.

Kiosks

My strongest suggestion is the kiosk venture. This is a lot more affordable and easier to manage. However, if you are making your own product, as I was for my gel candle design venture, be prepared to be up all night making them or have a backup plan. You never know how much you are going to sell on any day. I found myself making a hundred candles a night and bringing them to the mall the next day. It was a great time to sell my candles. They were new to the market and people loved them. They were a novelty item and it was the season to sell.

For a small, initial venture, the mall kiosks aren't too risky. You sell your products on the spot, and it's an easy way to test the market so I will expand further in the next section.

The ins and outs of kiosks and carts

Leasing a kiosk or cart is one of the best ways to introduce your consumer product to market or to sell a product you believe in. The least expensive kiosk option is to rent a cart at a mall for a short term to see how it goes. The response will be a good indication as to whether or not your product is going to attract sufficient interest from the public to make it seem reasonable to pursue its manufacturing and eventual marketing.

It's an affordable way to begin. Having a kiosk eliminates the overhead of a traditional storefront, and you are brought face-to-face with your customers.

It's up to you to attract customers so you can show off what you have. Being right there in the flow of foot traffic allows you to talk with the folks who pass by. Your conversation doesn't even need to be about selling them a product, as long as it calls their attention to what you have for sale. Be personable and friendly. If they don't happen to purchase anything immediately they are more likely to come back to a pleasant person. According to entrepreneur.com, the Mall of America has 40 million visitors a year and 100 temporary kiosks. That's a lot of customers available for a small price compared to storefront fees

(Source: entrepeneur.com/article/63012).

HINT: Just make sure typical mall customers will be interested in your product.

Cost of a mall kiosk

There are different types of leasing agreements and it depends on the needs of the mall. A variety of options can include weekly, monthly, seasonally and/or annually.

Costs vary by demand so popular times of the year and areas in good locations with higher footfall will cost more. Some prices could range between $2,500 to $10,000 per month (less when things aren't so great). Be prepared to negotiate for a better deal, especially off-season.

Kiosks are bigger than carts and offer certain luxuries you may not need if you have small and untried products. The carts are much cheaper and make it easy to present your product. Ask the mall management to show you the different options and you can then evaluate what works best for you. Remember that kiosks are much larger than carts so they will cost more and cut into your margins. You may be looking at as much as $9,000 to $10,000 per month.

My latest venture was a Mother's Day cart. I paid $1,500 for the month in a prime location. I think this was a steal, especially for Mother's Day, although you really don't need the whole month, only ten days prior to the big event, which is when you will make the largest share of your sales. Last-minute shoppers are the best, because price is far less important than attractiveness.

In my case they asked for a $500 down payment and the balance when I came in. If you only have enough for a down payment, you could ask if you can arrange to pay the rent toward the middle of the month. The malls I have been in always let me do that: down payment, then final payment on the 15th. Some malls will work with you. Contracts typically begin on the first of a month. Some malls take either the set price or 15% of sales, whichever is greater.

Visit the mall before you finalize your decision. Go at different times and note the traffic and the demographics for the various areas. Some useful locations to check are the main entrance, the food court, and close to some of the busier stores. Look for any stores that sell similar products to what you will be offering. Location is key. You may want to invest a little more for a better location—it almost always pays off, provided you have a truly sellable product.

The first time I sold in a mall was in a very low traffic area. It was, however, a well-known, beautiful mall. The cost during Christmas was $10,000 for the month in a low-traffic area and we grossed $100,000 over a two-month period. Of course, Christmas is a major holiday. I can't imagine how much we would have grossed in a high traffic area. But then again, the cost of the location may have been significantly more. So you want to weigh your options and pay close attention to your budget. It is always better to clear *something*—even a small amount—rather than *nothing*.

Also, be aware of the best time to be in a mall to sell your products. You may consider a short-term lease to test your product during major holidays. I always found Christmas and Mother's Day to be the best holidays for the kinds of products I sold. Mother's Day is like a mini-Christmas. In fact, with the right product(s) it is possible to net just as much money in a much shorter period of time. Everyone is looking for a gift on Mother's Day! It is often as simple as having a product with the word "Mom" or "Mother" on it. Year after year this was so successful that I always sold out. You have to be working in the mall on Mother's Day itself however, as that will very likely be your biggest single day.

Be involved with your customers

One of the most important features of success is being involved with your customers. Work them. Get to know them. If you see someone looking at your products, move toward them and engage them in conversation. Say hello and ask if they are looking for anything special. Find out what they are looking for and see if you could accommodate them or suggest something similar. Greet people who are walking by. Be friendly. Smile. Ask them for their opinion on your product. Don't be afraid to ask them to look. The worst they could do is say no or give you negative information. Learn from whatever response they may give you. Customers are the key to your success, so knowing their response to your product and its presentation is important to your bottom line.

Casual browsers don't become buyers all by themselves. Determine what they are looking at and perhaps pick it up and take it to them for close-up examination. You have to be willing to attract potential customers by working them—showing and telling them about your products.

Holiday season is by far the best time to be in a mall. However, if you find yourself loving the kiosk/cart business and you want to stay year round, you could build a loyal clientele. Develop a pipeline. Find ways to market to your regular customers, which will entice them—reward them—to come back and purchase products from you. You could offer customization, coupons, special pricing, points, rewards for bringing new customers, and more.

Design your space

Presentation is everything. A clean, bright kiosk can be so inviting. You will want to display your products so attractively that it will give customers a reason to stop and shop. One of my biggest mistakes early on was putting too many products out at once. This created clutter. Once I cleared the clutter, the products were more easily seen and examined. If you have a product that comes in several colors, put out just one or two, but let those who seem interested know that you have the others too if they might better fit their needs.

My recommendation is that you spend lots of time walking around the mall. Get some ideas from other kiosk/cart owners. Watch how the customers react to their products and displays.

Usually the carts at the mall will give you ample lighting and materials in their basic flat-rate service. There is often an array of options, however, and which you choose will depend on your budget. You don't have to start out elaborately. You could work your way up. Use the cart as it is if you have to, and add displays as you go. Initially I used the cart without adding any type of display so I know there is a difference to how customers respond.

Each mall has different types of carts. The first cart I used was awesome. I didn't have to add a thing. The shelving and the lighting were just right. With the next cart I had, I wasn't so lucky, however. Although it had great lighting, it was completely flat. I started with it just like that. I laid my products out on the flat surface and added shelving to it as I made money. I eventually added all-glass shelving. It was quite pretty and just right for my products. I sold mostly glass products and the glass shelving units added so much glamor.

I would never have known about glass shelving and how easy it was to use if it hadn't been for a cart next to me. I ended up buying the pieces from him. I used glass shelves with clips that held everything together, making a very sturdy display. I have found that you can purchase similar products on the web at www.acmedisplay.com. If you search the internet you may find other resources as well. Garage sales are a good place to look for shelving too. I recommend you go for just one kind of shelf. It offers a neater, more unified, professional look.

If you want or need more lighting and it is in your budget, LED lighting will provide the means to a nice bright and clean-looking cart. There are options for solid or flashing lights.

There are examples of kiosks/carts on the internet under 'mall cart displays' so do your research and find out what is available. Remember everything you do has to be approved by the mall and they will review your display plan and any lighting.

Basic mall requirements

In this section I list all the requirements that I have faced and you will most likely need to meet if you go down this route of working in a mall.

Application process

Ask at the mall office for a way to apply and they will let you know about pricing, deposits, and any additional information they need for the application. Make sure you understand about the complete costs you will be charged and the regulations you need to follow. Ask the mall how much deposit they require and when it is to be paid. Also check about key money. Ask about hours and mandatory requirements for the kiosk/cart to be manned.

You will need liability **insurance and signage.** Malls can provide you with information about both so ask for help if you need it.

You may have to show **photos** or **samples** of your work and present a drawing on how you plan on displaying your products.

At the kiosk itself

You will have to post your prices where customers can easily read them and a **returns policy**.

City and county regulations

You may require an occupational **license**. Check with your local city and county for any occupational **license** you may require. If you are a food vendor, certain licenses will be required and the rules will be very different. You can find this information directly from the mall management.

Tax information

You may need a Federal and a State tax **ID number**. You can obtain the former from the IRS, or use your social security number unless you intend to hire employees. The State Tax ID is for sales tax and you can get it online.

Mall security

As well as customers, malls may also be a place for opportunists who see your products as something they want to obtain without payment. An important duty is to protect yourself and your employees. Be aware of your surroundings at all times. Know where the exits are located and where to exit in case evacuation is required. Learn the mall security features as well as any special instructions when it comes to an emergency.

People can be a big help to you, especially those you see every day, so get to know your fellow kiosk workers and the security guards walking around the mall. Keep security phone numbers in a handy place. Post them on your register and keep them available for your employees.

If you participate in accepting mall gift certificates, make sure the ones customers hand you are real. Get an exact image copy from the mall office so you know what to look for. If you accept checks, be prepared to get stuck with a bad one. Be sure to run your credit cards on the spot for approval before you give your product away.

Equipment

There are specific items you will need at your kiosk or cart to run your business. The most important is a way for your customers to pay. You can accept cash and checks or you can accept cash and credit cards only.

If you accept checks, be aware of the risks involved. Checks could bounce and there is always a risk of fraud, which peaks at holiday times.

If you accept credit cards, be sure to get set up with a reputable company. Your bank may also offer this service. It is worth paying a little extra for this service as it will bring you more customers, and the customers it brings you tend to spend more than those sorting through the limited stash of cash in their wallets.

If you aren't familiar with the process, credit card service is called 'merchant services.' There are many different products out there enabling you to accept credit cards, such as mobile devices, scanners, and phone applications. Be sure to have one or more of these processes set up. Back in the day when I was running my kiosk, the technology wasn't out there. I used old-fashioned manual machines. When the day was over, I went home to close out the batch. I got stuck with quite a few bad credit cards. So be sure to get approval prior to handing over your product.

You will also need a cash register. You can purchase these very reasonably from a number of local retailers including Walmart, Office Depot, or Office Max. You don't need anything elaborate. All you need is a simple cash register to ring up your items and to keep track of what you have sold.

Sometimes the mall will supply you with the basic needs, but sometimes they want an extra fee, so be sure to find out up front. You will want a waste basket, pens and paper or maybe a laptop or portable device to track your customers. Remember you want to start building a pipeline of customers, so business cards or some kind of informative handout is essential. You will also want to have paper towels and glass cleaner to keep everything spotless. You may also need shopping bags or some form of packaging for your products. You should receive a key to lock up your belongings when you are not around them.

Lessons learned

- Do an internet search for samples of existing business plans related to your field.
- My strongest recommendation is for you to get a patent. The utility patent is one of the strongest patents out there.
- If you are looking for a manufacturer or a license agreement, be sure to have them sign a non-disclosure agreement, even if you have a patent pending.
- Calculate your profits to ensure you are working within your margins.
- Keep money for taxes separate from operating costs.
- Having a kiosk eliminates the overhead of a traditional storefront, and you are brought face-to-face with your customers.
- Make sure typical mall customers will be interested in your product.
- Always run your entire display plans (and any subsequent changes) by the mall officials before you invest in material or even sign your lease.

PART 4

Providing Goods for Resale

Benefits of providing goods for resale

Winning a contract to sell to a big company can be just what you need to grow your business, but there are certain things you need to be aware of if you want to compete successfully with the rest that are trying to do the same thing.

As I've mentioned, I started out selling my gel candle designs through the kiosk and cart route in malls. I sold to individuals passing by and that led to big sales during peak times such as Mother's Day. Perhaps, like me, you also have a product that has sold really well in small quantities and you now want to expand your sales to the big stores. You are ready to sell in bulk and are not sure what to do next or where to go for information. Well, I'm here to help.

Whether you are an independent candle designer trying to pitch that successful first order to a retail giant like Walmart or a small food industry firm trying to get your foot in the door with catering and supplies to a TV production crew, getting that vote of confidence through your first big order can be a game changer for your company and the way you do business.

Not only will you be making more money, if all goes well, but working with large firms will boost the image of your firm for other big businesses and will provide you with the confidence and know how to be able to replicate your success and grow as a company. You will find it easier to sell to other big companies, once you've sold to one, so don't waste this opportunity by attempting it unprepared.

However, there are obstacles and challenges you need to meet when you deal with bigger clients. You need to make sure you have large amounts of stock available and be able to deliver when they want you to, and this can place a bit strain on your business.

Goods and services fall under different categories and one of your main priorities will be to make sure that you follow the requirements that are attached to each type of product. General goods do not involve goods sold to children and indeed the latter will have stricter requirements.

Before you start trying to sell, make sure that you know where to look for information and familiarize yourself with what you have to check against. I have put together a list of what you may come across. The most important thing is to ask and research first, about where you want to sell and what they need from you. There is no point doing all your own research and work, spending a lot of money on patents, development, production and marketing, only to find out that suppliers won't buy from you because you've failed to meet their requirements.

Things to keep in mind:

Returns

Find out what the company's policy is on returns and ensure that you establish an agreement that suits you. It is common for retailers to return any products that they cannot sell or that customers return to them. You can't predict what will sell or how customers will behave with complete accuracy so be prepared to deal with this.

Detail

If the company is going to advertise your product (or products) then make sure that you know how they will be promoting it. Ask to see the marketing material, and that includes anything that is in print or that will go online. Send them the correct details that describe your product.

In the next section we take a look at some of the requirements you need to look out for and we go through some case studies of some big companies.

Requirements for suppliers providing goods for resale

Food Suppliers
Food Safety Requirements

If you are a company that sells edible products you will need to check with your supplier as to how you can meet their food safety requirements. Expect more complicated requests than if you are selling non-edible merchandise.

An onsite audit of a food factory

Some suppliers will request an onsite audit of any food factory you are using. You may be able to have this done by a third party and use that certification for any supplier.

At time of writing, an onsite audit can range in cost from $975 to $1,250 depending on the location of the facility. You will need a General Certificate of Conformity (GCC).

The most basic part of an onsite audit is having an auditor visit your premises and inspect the safety and suitability of your production facilities. You will be informed of when the visit will take place and when your auditor will arrive. They may, at that point, let you know about the schedule in which the process will proceed.

Variation in the audit will be dependent on the site of your premises and what you produce. Auditors will have their own standards so this is a general glance so you know what to expect. As always, you will benefit from researching the process and what other companies have experienced.

Once the auditor arrives, there will be an initial meeting to discuss what happens next. It would be a good idea to have any staff from the factory in attendance. The auditor(s) will want to see the production areas and where the activities and general manufacturing process occur. They will look through your systems and want to check all of your paperwork. Make sure you have everything ready. Missing paperwork about safety and regulations can be harmful to your score. The auditor will write up their experience and collate the evidence they have observed. There will then be a closing meeting.

The aim of the audit is to check your processes and the systems put in place. During the process the auditor may find problems that don't comply with the health and safety requirements. At the end of the audit you will be made aware of things that need to be fixed in order to meet the criteria of the certification board. You will receive a report and information about what, if anything, needs to be done next.

Note that if anything critical or illegal is discovered, you may have to stop production until any problem is corrected. Some critical problems will result in certification not being issued.

(Source: http://www.brcglobalstandards.com/Manufacturers/Food/Gettingstarted/AuditandCertification.aspx#.VSZexvnF81I)

Pack House

A Pack House is a covered location where you can keep perishable goods until they are ready to sell. After a harvest, for example, you need to prepare your fruit and vegetables. You can either do this on the farm itself or once the products have been delivered to their destination, whether that be retail stores, wholesale locations or the supermarkets. If you expect to provide goods and foods for retailers then you will need to certify your pack house as meeting their standards as well. (Source: Food and Agriculture Organization of the United Nations website, http://www.fao.org/docrep/008/y4893e/y4893e05.htm)

Dealing with specific companies

I want to show you, now, what specific retail stores will ask of you and where to find the information. The particular store you want to work with may not be discussed here but the following will show you what to look out for and you can extrapolate from that.

Case study 1 - Walmart

Walmart is the biggest retailer in the US and one of the biggest stores in the world with international reach and huge buying power. In 2013, Walmart had over 4000 stores in the US but had over 6000 overseas. If you're not looking to sell your products through them yet, then you may start thinking about them as one of your options for the future. Their revenue in 2014 was six times that of their next competitor, Target, in the 'general merchandise' category, and came in at $476 million (source: Fortune 500).

They provide the most relevant information you will need as a new business working with them, on their corporate website:

http://corporate.walmart.com/suppliers/minimum-requirements

Food regulations

They specify that all companies that provide edible products and want to become a supplier to them, must meet their food and safety requirements. Walmart source food globally so it's important that they can ensure the security of their food chain. The following are some of the steps needed to ensure this.

New Food Factories

Before Walmart will buy from you, you must request an onsite audit of the food factory you are using. You do this through the website Retail Link which is where you have to log in with the credentials you used to sign up. You need to do this before you put in a purchase order with the retailer. The cost when I last checked was in the range of $975 to $1,250 depending on where the facility is located.

Pack House

Just like with any food factory, if you are using a Pack House then you need to make sure that you fulfil the requirements that Walmart requires. In the first instance of working with the retailer, your pack house will need to go through and complete a "Pre-Assessment Checklist for Pack Houses" before you can issue any purchase orders.

You will also need to request an onsite audit of the pack house through Retail Link in the same manner as you did with the food factory. The cost is the same as for food factories.

Note: Walmart will accept the official security audit results of any pack house or food factory that has been audited on behalf of another retailer by any Walmart authorized third party audit firm, and has received a passing score of 71 or above. If the facility failed the audit, it will not be accepted and the facility must undergo a Walmart security audit.

Retail Link

Once you have signed a Supplier Agreement with Walmart you will be assigned a supplier number. You will then be given information about Retail Link and a Retail Link Access Request Form. Fill in the form and return it to the Retail Link team.

Retail Link is a 'decision support system' and a service that connects you, the supplier, to Walmart, and you can access it through the web.

Retail Link lets you retrieve the sales and inventory data of your items and you can find out up-to-date information on any developments for your sales. Purchase orders can be downloaded via Retail Link too. The website address is https://retaillink.wal-mart.com .

General Merchandise Suppliers

Product Safety and Compliance is responsible for General Merchandise in all U.S. and Puerto Rico retail formats for Walmart, Walmart.com, Sam's Club, and Samsclub.com. Food and Pharmacy are covered by different groups within Walmart. You will need to contact different departments if you want to deal with those goods.

Product quality and product safety and regulations are two different things so while Walmart provide information regarding product safety and regulatory requirements they do not include requirements related to product quality. It is your responsibility to ascertain product quality.

GTIN/UPC Membership Number

Walmart requires the global trade item number (GTIN) / Universal Product Code (UPC) on your application documents. The initial fee is approximately $760. To get started, visit www.gs1us.org or call (866) 280-4013.

Note: These requirements DO NOT apply to Service and Non-Resale Suppliers.

Product Safety and Compliance

Product Safety and Compliance administers programs to identify, mitigate and monitor risks associated with general merchandise. For that reason, Walmart require submission of all product test reports, as well as the General Certificates of Conformity (GCC).

Global Merchandise and Apparel

A new factory, regardless of the global location, the Walmart retail market, or country risk rating, is required to pass an onsite supply chain security audit conducted by one of Walmart's appointed audit firms prior to being activated in Retail Link.

Factory Capability & Capacity Assessment (FCCA) Audit

A Factory Capability and Capacity Audit (FCCA) is required prior to order commitment for new factories of all suppliers classification and retails markets.

High-priced products often require anti-theft tagging. If this applies to your products, contact ADT/Sensormatic at (877)-258-6424 or <u>sourcetag@sensormatic.com</u>.

Case study 2 - QVC

QVC is a TV shopping network, not to be confused with The Home Shopping Network, which is a different business but very similar in style. The original goal for both companies was to give buyers access to their products by watching the channels on TV and then ordering products that have just been presented.

QVC gets shown in 250 million homes across the world while the Home Shopping Network has an audience reach spanning 90 million homes. They also sell across the internet and through smartphones, whether through iPhones or Android. There are very few ways to reach that many people and sell a lot of products so quickly, through your six to seven minute slot.

To who will you be selling your product? QVC say that the demographic profile of their customers "span all socio-economic groups and varies significantly on the products being aired. For instance, a cooking program attracts both sexes, whereas a fashion hour has a mainly female viewership."

Watching the TV channel is a way of exploring their catalogue. They have spent years building up an audience for their products and accessing that supply of consumers would be a big advantage for your company. However, there are issues you need to be aware of before you start selling to them.

Inventory

First of all, you will need a significant investment to be able to supply the inventory that QVC will require. As a company with a large number of customers, they need to make sure that when people request your product, they are able to meet that demand. They ensure that they have enough inventory in stock to satisfy a great deal of potential buyers.

What does this mean for you? You need to make sure that you have the capabilities to a) manufacture the quantity demanded of you; and b) be able to ship enough inventory to them in order for them to satisfy the market demand. You need to be able to do this before you appear on the show.

You only get paid if, or when, your product gets sold through QVC. So if no one wants to buy what you advertise on your presentation slot then you'll end up with a lot of inventory that will have cost you a fair amount of money to produce. Make sure that you know the risks going into this process and ensure that you can afford to keep working if you don't manage to sell through QVC. Choosing the route of the TV shopping network is an expensive one for a small company but it can be worthwhile.

One of the riskier aspects of QVC, their requirement for a lot of inventory, can also be an advantage because their large customer base means they are always looking for new products to feature in their brief slots. Presenting and selling on these networks could be a great opportunity if your product is suitable. If you can present it in a pleasing way and if it is designed to sell to a broad audience rather than a small niche market then you have a great chance for it to be a success (source: http://www.entrepreneur.com/article/168876).

Selling

To learn how to begin the process of selling on QVC you will first need to visit the website where you can find more information. Go to: http://vendorportal.qvc.com/SitePages/Home.aspx for the vendor information. The first step involves making an appointment with a QVC buyer to show off your product. The QVC headquarters are in West Chester, Pennsylvania, but there are appointments available across the country and you can apply for those according to your location. You can also apply online and if they are interested they will get in touch for further information about presenting your product.

QVC look for a wide variety of products that can be demonstrated effectively on-air. They are "particularly interested in exclusive product launches and unique merchandise which is being offered for the first time." Their programs usually last for an hour and have specific themes around which products are based for that time period.

The product ranges in which they are currently interested include the following:

Women's apparel & accessories (including shoes), beauty, bed & bath, consumer electronics, food, gifts,

82

handbags/luggage, health & fitness, hobby & craft, home décor, home improvement, home textiles, household cleaners, jewelry, kitchen gadgets, kitchen electrical goods, patio and garden, plants, personal care and storage (source: Vendor's Guide, QVC).

QVC do not sell items that fall under the following categories: Feminine/personal hygiene, firearms, fuel additives, gambling–related products, genuine furs, sexual aids, or tobacco–related products.

Products that are highly demonstrable, solve problems, make life easier, appeal to a broad audience, and have unique features and benefits are of interest to QVC.

Another thing to look out for is the price range that QVC like to work with. Check whether the price of your product fits in with what they will sell, whether it be a minimum or maximum price.

Other businesses

Target

If you would like to pitch your product to Target so that it can be stocked in their stores, they recommend you call their Target Vendor Hotline on (612) 696-7500.

Costco

Prospective vendors of non-food or sundry items can contact the corporate office at the addresses below. Costco's corporate mailing address is:

PO Box 34331
Seattle, WA 98124
Costco's corporate offices are located at:
999 Lake Drive
Issaquah, WA 98027

Prospective vendors of food and sundry items can contact the appropriate division office. Check online for further details:
http://www.costco.com/vendor-inquiries.html

Big Lots Inc.

Big Lots provide all the requirements that they need from their vendors online at the following website: http://www.biglots.com/corporate/vendor-relations/vendor-routing-and-compliance . You can find information there about purchase orders, retail ordering systems and all sorts of different standards for the products they will accept.

Burlington Stores Inc.

Burlington Stores provide information and access to their dealings with vendors, through the following website: http://www.burlingtoncoatfactory.com/vendors

PART 5

Real-Life Experiences as Case Studies

I'll start by sharing experiences I know about and you can send in your own as well. You will find contact details at the end of the book.

The next section expands on two examples of how to run a company by starting up a business. The first example is in the construction industry and the second is in the food industry.

How to get involved with government construction jobs

I'm going to use an example from the construction trade in order to be more specific about how the available resources can help. My son and his friend started a flooring business and obtained many government jobs through a website called conexbuff.com. They paid to become part of the community and this has proven worth the cost.

The website offers an email service which sends out updated jobs listings. In the case of my son and his partner, they first searched the database for epoxy flooring and fluid apply flooring. From that point on they received emails from the construction exchange along with the specifications of that particular job or jobs. Each job was divided into business categories and they picked flooring which gave them the exact description of what the client needed and what they wanted done. It also shows what products they want to be used. They would pull up a blueprint and figure out a cost with a program they use.

Not all jobs are state and not all are federal on this website so be sure to read all the details. There are requirements to be aware of:

- There need to be up to 20 contractors submitting a bid to the contractor (the General Contractor).
- The General Contractor puts together all the prices and then they submit their bid to the state or federal. You may need to discuss your bid and if the job is accepted then you win your section of the contract.

My son's partner made $60,000 in his first year working for an epoxy floor company and saw how profitable it could be. He next got a black topping job with another company and started doing garage floors on the weekends. He started to get more jobs and some were much bigger. His first big job was worth $50,000 and it started to get serious.

Right around that time, a friend of his who used to work with him in the business gave him some really old equipment for about $1000. His work was so good, he kept getting big jobs. In the beginning his brother helped him with a few of those jobs but at some point couldn't help him anymore. That is when he called my son in to help him with the business and they went into the flooring business together. They are still doing it today, winning bids and being very successful.

HINT: Make sure you enter into a partnership agreement.

They started out with one piece of small equipment, purchased more equipment from a friend, worked their way up and added some new equipment worth $50,000 to $100,000. Some of the types of jobs they got include an aircraft base which provided enough money for the purchase of a $20,000 grinder. They found a way to access information about what jobs were available and are now doing well.

In the construction business, the key thing is making connections with certain people, specifically, general contractors, and when you work for them make sure you do a good job.

However, it is a very risky business which could be very expensive if, and when, you or others mess up. If you are good at what you do, then you become less of a risk and more general contractors will use you.

The Construction Exchange is where you make connections and get on good terms. Your competition makes for a good source of contacts because when they don't want to or can't do a job, they will know who to contact to do it for them.

You may come across some heavier competition but you could still work with them to help each other out. Small companies may struggle with jobs worth over two million dollars and larger businesses have high costs associated with employing personnel. You have to look at each job to see what the prevailing rate is for that job plus any benefits your workers have to have in place. You base your bid on all of this.

Another useful site for builders is the Builders Exchange in Florida.

http://www.builderex.com/ipin/about.htm. You can find some in your area through a search for builders' connection in a search engine.

Tips in starting a restaurant

Another example we can look at is the restaurant industry. Since I have been writing this book, my husband sub-leased a space in a gas station to sell food. He decided to sell subs and sandwiches. He has a background in this industry so it wasn't an unknown for him.

The venture started with looking for equipment, used on Craigslist to begin with. We ended up getting a proofer for making our own bread, a commercial toaster oven, a slicer, and a large deli case. There was already a hand-sink and a counter in place and the store allowed us to use their freezer. We just had to purchase a couple of tables. There was also a three-bay sink and mop sink in the back room which we were able to use (a mandatory requirement for a restaurant).

As restaurant owners, we registered for membership with Restaurant Depot for our food. You just need to show them your sales tax number (available from the state's website) and a copy of your county business license (local county clerk's office).

The following are some if not most of the things needed when opening a restaurant. You will need everything in place before you get your inspection for your food permit.

- A tax / business license, from the County Clerk's Office;
- A sales tax number, from the secretary of state website;
- A federal tax ID number, from the IRS website (irs.gov);
- Registration of your business, from the secretary of state website or county clerk's office for DBA (Doing Business As). This depends on how you are going to set up the business whether it be as a sole proprietor, corporation, or LLC;
- You need to take the food manager/handling course, to learn about the food temperature and storage requirements;
- You need to have a "Choking" sign posted;
- Keep everything clean;
- Keep all your food labeled with correct expiration dates. You will learn how to date your food from the food safety course.

Once everything is in place, contact the department of agriculture for inspection and once you pass, you will get a temporary license to post until the original one is mailed to you. The Fire Department may also have to come out for an inspection if you plan on deep frying. If you sell packaged foods, ask the Department of Agriculture for information.

PART 6

Summing Up

Don't give up

I have gone through all you are about to go through, so I know you will need perseverance and patience. Here is one of my last but most important pieces of advice: Don't give up.

As I stated earlier, my patented product was a form, so I researched the print and form industry. I started with distributors and worked my way back to manufacturers. I was totally unfamiliar with the industry. So if you are, or can easily become, even a little familiar, you are that much further ahead of where I was. My form needed special glue, so I had to search for glue manufacturers. Depending on your product, you will need to research, research, and research.

I was lucky enough (or unlucky enough) to find a manufacturer that manufactured that product and also marketed their products to their distributors.

For my gel candle product, I chose to market in the mall which proved to be very successful. It depends on your product where and how you market.

Don't give up! If one manufacturer can't do it, another one can. If you can't find a manufacturer to make your product, make it yourself.

Keep the flame burning!

Stay excited. Keep looking. Keep moving forward. If you believe in your product, you can find someone to produce it. Remember when you find someone to make sure you enter into a formal written agreement with them. Remember, don't give them an exclusive arrangement. You need room for growth and expansion. By limiting yourself to one manufacturer, you are limiting your success and increasing your chances of losing the product.

Don't back off once the product is on the market. Stay with it and know what is going on every step of the way. There are actually two journeys: one to bring your product to market and the other to stay involved once it is on the market.

Keep control of your product

I came up with a few manufacturers who were interested and I ended up going with just one because I was bullied into it. Learn from my mistakes. Don't give up control of your product. Stay involved and make it a partnership. Most manufacturers already have a list of distributors who they sell to, so you too may be able to cut a deal with them to market your product to their clients. Again, don't give them total control over your product.

By following my processes, you could market your own product through gift and trade shows, trade organizations, kiosks and carts, etc. You could go from state to state to introduce it. Once you get manufacturers lined up, I can only stress that you must stay on top of things so you know what's happening on all your playing fields. Don't be bullied and don't trust anyone in business. Get everything in writing, and yes, have an attorney review it for you. This is your deal and your product.

Don't be taken for a sucker

Don't trust anyone in business. Make sure you have an attorney to protect your rights. You've worked hard on your invention so don't be bullied out of it. Keep the faith and keep moving forward. Be careful and cover all your steps. Make as much money as you can, when you can. More than likely, if it is really good, somebody will try and steal it from you. That's sad but it's the truth.

I was lucky for a while. I found ways to get around the havoc. I had a Fortune 500 company standing behind me initially so it was easy for me to stop other manufacturers from making the product. My biggest mistake was my placing trust in, and giving the Kansas Company, an exclusive agreement. I put my faith and hope in our partnership but failed myself when I didn't follow through with a signed agreement. Get something in writing and don't put a time limit on your agreement. This is your product and you are partnering together to bring it to market. Why should someone else take your credit?

How's your story going to go?

I really want to see you succeed and hear all about it. I am here for each of you so here is my challenge. When you have a story to tell me, put fingers to keyboard and let me know at my personal email address:

Km2688@gmail.com. My website can be your platform to tell others as well, so I am happy to post your experiences. Let's all learn together. I want my mistakes to be for your gain and everything you do will make it all worth it.

Take advantage of all the tools listed in this book. Review the sites that were introduced to you and get familiar with the process. Visit the USPTO.gov website to keep up with the patent laws and current forms and fees. Visit the SBA website to familiarize yourself with the tools to run a business. Check out trade shows and your local malls to see what they charge for kiosks, and always ask about any special deals they may be able to offer you. Begin the process with the idea of having fun and then go have some!

So now it's your turn.

GO GET 'EM!

References

www.uspto.gov - United States Patent Office

www.sba.gov - Small Business Association

www.builderex.com - Builders Exchange NY

www.google.com - Search Engine

www.acmedisplay.com – Acme Display

www.mbda.gov - Minority Business Development Centers

www.Legalzoom.com -Legal Zoom

www.builderex.com/ipin/about.htm - Builders Exchange

www.irs.gov – Internal Revenue Service

www.safewayclasses.com/floridappc/florida.html - Professional Food Handler Certifications

www.sba.gov/content/develop-cash-flow-analysis-your-business - Develop a cash flow analysis

www.marketingdonut.co.uk/marketing/sales/sales-lead-generation/selling-to-big-business - Selling to big business

There is a useful diagram which outlines the process for obtaining a utility patent at the following URL:

http://www.uspto.gov/patents/process/index.jsp and one on how to maintain it:

http://www.uspto.gov/patents/process/maintain.jsp

APPENDIX I

Patents

Maintaining Your Patent

Once you obtain a utility patent you need to maintain it in force through a set of maintenance fees. These fees will need to be paid three times over the life of the patent and are subject to the following schedule:

- Three to three and a half years after the date of issue for the first payment;
- Seven to seven and a half years after the date of issue for the second payment; and
- 11 to 11 and a half years after the date of issue for the third and final payment.

For further information and surcharges see the USPTO.gov website.

APPENDIX II

Food Safety

Each state has its own food safety division which is responsible for making sure that the food supply is wholesome and healthy by enforcing the food safety laws. When you're looking to find what laws and regulations are appropriate for your food business then the Food Safety Division in each state is the best place to start.

I have provided the following two examples so you can see what you should expect to find:

    1. Florida Food Safety Division

The Division of Food Safety is responsible for assuring the public of a safe, wholesome, and properly represented food supply through permitting and inspection of food establishments, inspection of food products, and performance of specialized laboratory analyses on a variety of food products sold or produced in the state. The division monitors food from farm gate through processing and distribution to the retail point of purchase (http://www.freshfromflorida.com/Divisions-Offices/Food-Safety).

The division is charged with administration and enforcement of the food and poultry and egg laws, and also provides support in the enforcement of other food safety laws. In addition to regulatory surveillance and enforcement, the division evaluates consumer complaints related to food.

2. Georgia Department of Agriculture

"Our Food Safety Division administers state laws, rules and regulations for retail and wholesale grocery stores, retail seafood stores and places in the business of food processing and plants which are currently required to obtain a license from the Commissioner under any other provision of law: bakeries, confectioneries, fruit, nuts, and vegetables stores and places of business, and similar establishments, mobile or permanent, engaged in sale of food primarily for consumption off the premises. This does not include "food service establishments" (Restaurants and Institutions - http://agr.georgia.gov/foodsafety.aspx).

The Department of Agriculture in Georgia provides a list of all planning permits and regulations you will need for food safety: http://www.freshfromflorida.com/Divisions-Offices/Food-Safety. The information ranges from egg law regulations to working in community kitchens.

APPENDIX III

Federal Licenses & Permits

The Small Business Advisory service is a great place to find information and I want to list some of the topics you can access and tell you where to find them. Often you don't know what is required until you need to provide it and that is where research comes in handy. There is no need to reinvent the wheel.

How Do You Know if You Need A License or a Permit?

There are two issues that you need to assess when investigating whether you need a license:

1. In what type of industry will you be working?
2. Are the activities regulated locally or federally?

Types of industry

If you are interested in selling alcohol or dealing with firearms or commercial fishing then your activities are supervised and regulated by a federal agency so you will need to obtain a federal license or permit. However, it is not so simple. Alcoholic beverages, for example, are covered both federally and locally. To manufacture, wholesale, import, or sell alcoholic beverages, you will need to register your business and obtain federal permits. You will also need to contact your local Alcohol Beverage Control Board for local alcohol business permit and

100

licensing information (see Appendix V for more information).

The following is a list of more businesses:

Agriculture – relevant if you import or transport animals, animal products, biologics, biotechnology, or plants across state lines.

Aviation – if your business involves the operation of aircraft or the use of aircraft in goods transport or aircraft maintenance.

Firearms, Ammunition, and Explosives – any work in this business means you need to comply with the Gun Control Act's licensing requirements.

Fish and Wildlife – this is relevant if you are involved with any wildlife related activity.

Maritime Transportation – this is for business providing ocean transportation or any shipment of cargo by sea.

Mining and Drilling – any drilling for natural resources.

Nuclear Energy – for any production of nuclear energy.

Radio and Television Broadcasting – for any business broadcasts over radio, television, wire, satellite, or cable.

Transportation and Logistics – If you operate an oversize or overweight vehicle you will need a permit.
(Source: http://www.sba.gov/content/what-federal-licenses-and-permits-does-your-business-need)
SBA have a search tool called Permit Me that will help you find general business permits, licenses, and registrations required by your state, county or city.

APPENDIX IV

Finances

Estimating Startup Costs

I don't have the answers for how much your business will cost but I can help you find the tools to estimate your own requirements based on your needs. This amount of budgetary knowledge and awareness will not only look great in your business plan but also help you get started.

Some things to think about are whether you need inventory or equipment or whether you can start with minimal investment. Property and renovation costs are things to consider, as well as long-term versus short-term lease or purchase of goods.

Here are some things to consider that you will need to establish for your first few months:

- One-time costs
  - Leasing your property
  - Incorporating your business
  - Obtaining equipment
- On-going costs
  - Utilities
  - Insurance
  - Staff

Identify which of these costs are essential and which aren't and then stick to only the essentials, at least to begin with. Use a worksheet and keep a list of your costs under those categories, on-going and one-time.

(Source: http://www.sba.gov/content/estimating-startup-costs)

Using Personal Finances

While you spend your time sorting out the finances for your business, don't forget to assess your own personal finances too. Your household expenses will still be there once you're running and pouring all of your money into your work.

Prioritize your personal finances and make sure you can keep going. Some tips on doing this are as follows:

1. Write a personal monthly budget for your household expenses
   - Be conservative
2. Check your personal credit history
   - Obtain a credit report from a credit bureau. The three major credit bureaus are: Equifax, Experian, and TransUnion.

(Source: http://www.sba.gov/content/using-business-vs-personal-finances)

Preparing Financial Statements

Some financial statements that will help your business are the balance sheet and the income statement. You will need these in your business plan so here is some brief help to understand them. Check online with the SBA for more detailed information.

Balance Sheet - The balance sheet is a snapshot of your business's finances. It establishes your assets, liabilities, and your net worth. These elements need to be listed. Taken over time, the state of these elements will reflect on the progress of your business. It will help you understand how you are doing and what you need to do in the future and also provide evidence to anyone else examining the business.

The source of your business's funds comes from the state of your liabilities and your net worth. They represent your creditors and investors, even if the only investor is you.

Assets – Assets are things of value including cash or credit.

Liabilities – Liabilities are your obligations and have to be met.

Current Assets are valid for less than a year's time. They include cash and any money outstanding.

There is more information about Cash, Accounts Receivable (A/R), Inventory, Notes Receivable (N/R), Other Current Assets, Fixed Assets, Intangibles such as Research and Development and Patents online at SBA. You will also find extensive information about all different types of liabilities and income as well.

(Source: http://www.sba.gov/content/financial-statements)

Developing a Cash Flow Analysis

Your cash flow analysis should also go in your business plan so this is a very useful thing for your business.

Any cash coming into the business is your inflow and is what you'll get as a result of selling your goods, any loans or credit and selling off any assets. Anything you pay will be your outflow. The combination of inflow and outflow is the cash flow for your business.

It is important to maintain a source of cash for your business at all times in order to meet your operational costs and any unforeseen problems that may come up.

Keeping an eye on your cash flow will help you predict your future cash flow as well and give validity to your future projections for your business.

In your business plan you will be able to show any changes over time to your cash flow and any net cash availability.

There are three sections that are usually covered: operating activities, investment activities, and financing activities.

(Source: http://www.sba.gov/content/develop-cash-flow-analysis-your-business)

Breakeven Analysis

The breakeven point happens when your revenue equals all your business costs. Your breakeven analysis will let you know and let your shareholders and investors know, when your business can expect to make a profit.

You need to take into account your startup and on-going costs, and once you set them against incoming revenue you will know when you will start making a profit.

You will have your fixed costs that don't vary no matter how much you sell and need to be paid no matter what happens. Variable costs are dependent on volume of sale and you will have to take these into account as well.

A formula that will help you determine your breakeven point is the following:

Breakeven point = fixed costs / (unit selling price – variable costs)

(Source: http://www.sba.gov/content/breakeven-analysis)

Borrowing Money for Your Business

You may need to borrow money in order to get started or to keep going, so understanding how you will be assessed by the banks will help you know what information to provide and what your chances are of getting that additional help.

Banks evaluate requests based on the following: the type of financing you are requesting, your ability to repay, your credit history, equity investment, collateral, and your experience in managing a business.

Types of Financing – The amount of money you or others have put into your company is called equity. The more you have invested, i.e., the higher the ratio of your equity to debt, the more likely a bank will be to lend you money. The following information is also applicable to equity investment.

If you have a high debt to equity ratio, however, you may be better off seeking further investment or higher

106

equity in the business. You can do this through **Equity Financing** or raising money in exchange for selling a percentage of your business.

If you already have high equity in your business you can use **Debt Financing** and borrow money that you will then need to repay over a short or longer period of time. You don't relinquish any ownership of the business but you do pay interest in the loan. The loan may be secured against any assets the company has.

Ability to Repay – Your business's ability to repay is attached to any collateral the business may have and your cash flow. Since banks examine financial statements to assess any ability to repay, businesses that have been in existence for longer will be seen more favorable since they will be able to show evidence of their behavior.

Credit History – Your personal credit history will play a role in this assessment too, especially if your business is so new that it doesn't have a credit history of its own.

Collateral is what the bank will claim back if the loan cannot be repaid.

Management Experience – If you have previous experience of managing other businesses and have a proven track record then this will be seen favorably by the bank. The way a manager handles a business is a big factor in its success.

(Source: http://www.sba.gov/content/borrowing-money)

APPENDIX V

Liquor Laws

Here I am including information about what you will require if you want to obtain a liquor license for a bar or restaurant. This is intended to provide you with a flavor of requirements and different specifications according to federal and local legislation.

Liquor Laws and Licensing for Your Bar or Restaurant

Opening a bar may seem simple and an almost ubiquitous practice, there are, after all, bars everywhere. However, requirements are different from state to state so be aware that you will need to investigate your own local liquor laws.

The first agency you need to be aware of is the Department of Alcoholic Beverage Control (ABC). As they state, their mission is "to administer the provisions of the Alcoholic Beverage Control Act in a manner that fosters and protects the health, safety, welfare, and economic well-being of the people of the State." The Department's workload is divided into three elements: administration, licensing, and compliance. These agencies determine all the variables attached to liquor sales and use. For example, they determine the kinds of liquor that can be sold, business parameters such as hours of sale and when and where liquor can be sold. They determine and implement license fees, quotas, and requirements, such as qualifications, for obtaining a liquor license.

Qualifications to obtain a license will vary according to the state but some of the basic ones include being of legal drinking age and being resident in the same state.

Liquor laws often vary between cities, counties and states. It's important to inform yourself on exactly what your state and city require, and how to comply with all requisite laws.

Liquor Licenses and Permits

Your liquor license can take time to obtain so you need to plan for the wait. You cannot legally open a bar without it so you should put it as one of your first tasks.

Types of Liquor Licenses

The types of licenses and permits available are dependent on the state where you want to open your bar. For example, there are twenty-two liquor license classifications in New York including Drug Store Beer, Grocery Beer, and Ball Park Beer, so you need to find out what you require. It may be easier to obtain one type of permit over another. It may be easier for you to get a lawyer to deal with the process.

Drug store beer - Beer license for off-premises only by bona fide pharmacies (take out).

Grocery store beer - Beer license for off-premises only by bona fide groceries (take out).

Ball park beer - For on-premises consumption of beer at baseball parks, racetracks, and other athletic fields and stadia OTHER than those maintained by EDUCATIONAL Institutions.

(Source: Liquor Authority, New York State. https://www.sla.ny.gov/definition-of-license-classes)

Applying for a license

Your application to the appropriate governing body may take up to a year depending on whether there are any issues that you have to deal with. Check your local licensing branch of the ABC as they will have advice and information. See, for example, the frequently asked questions on the New York State website https://www.sla.ny.gov/frequently-asked-questions .

APPENDIX VI

SBA Financial Assistance Eligibility

One of the most vital resources for startup businesses is knowing where to get financial assistance. If you don't have the finances you simply can't run a company. The SBA provides financial assistance but you have to be eligible.

If you fit the following criteria you may be able to apply:

• Do you operate for profit?

• Are you engaged in, or are proposing to do business in, the United States or its possessions?

• Do you have reasonable owner equity to invest?

• Have you used alternative financial resources, including personal assets, before seeking financial assistance?

If your answers are yes, then I recommend you apply for the assistance. The help is out there and if you can benefit then do so. Make sure however that you don't fall under the following special considerations which apply to some businesses. They include the following:

• If your franchise is so strict in its regulation that you do not seem to have a right to profit from it.

• You cannot selectively deny or restrict the use of your facilities or clubs to any groups in society.

Go to the website for further information on exceptions to eligible businesses.

You won't be eligible if your business is of the following type: engaged in illegal activities, loan packaging, speculation, gambling, investment or lending, or if the owner is on parole. There are specific examples online if you are not sure whether your business falls under the above criteria.

(Source: http://www.sba.gov/content/sba-financial-assistance-eligibility)

Financial Literacy and Education Commission

In an attempt to bring financial literacy and education to people in the United States, the U.S. Small Business Administration (SBA) set up the Financial Literacy and Education Commission. The Commission has established a national financial education website at www.MyMoney.gov, a hotline (1-888-My Money), and a national strategy on financial education (source: http://www.sba.gov/moneysmart).

They have also created courses for small businesses. One of the courses I would recommend because of its important insight for those just starting out, is the Money Smart for Small Business. The course provides the tools and information for you to better manage your money for your business and it is available for free.

It provides introductory-style training for new and aspiring entrepreneurs in 10 modules. You will learn essential information on running a small business from a financial standpoint as well as learning about the basics, and setting you up for more advanced training and technical assistance.

The 10 modules include:

1. **Banking Services** – This will cover understanding the most common banking services for a small business, including business checking, payroll processing, business loan, and others.

2. **Organizational Types** – You will learn in more detail some of the benefits to using different company structures such as those I have already discussed: Sole proprietor, Partnerships, Limited liability Company (LLC), C-corporation, and S-corporation.

3. **Time Management** – You will learn about general time management practices such as Pareto Analysis, ABC Method, Eisenhower method, and POSEC method, while learning why they are important to your business.

4. **Financial Management** – You will learn about financing basics for small business, such as: start up financing, financing fixed asset, working capital. Understand why and how they are important and become familiarized with the tools, practices, and rules commonly available to businesses like yours.

5. **Record Keeping** – You will learn the basics about record keeping, including how to use common tools, and practices. You will also become familiar with software that can help you put your record keeping into practice.

6. **Credit Reporting** – You will learn about the credit reporting and its benefits, risks and responsibilities. You will find out how credit reports work and how they are used amongst businesses and, most importantly, how to improve your own business' credit.

7. **Risk Management** – Risk management will help you identify common risks relevant to a business such as yours; it helps you spot common risks and provide you with the tools to implement your own risk management plan.

8. **Insurance** – This module will help you understand why you need insurance and what types are available.

9. **Tax Planning and Reporting** – This is an essential module for those who have not encountered tax reporting before. The course offers information on the federal, state, and local tax reporting requirements of a small business. You will learn how to manage your obligations and maintain your accounts. You will also become familiar with the forms and processes required to manage your taxes.

10. **Selling a Small Business and Succession Planning** – This module will teach you how to sell and shut down a business and will also help you understand how to set up a retirement plan.

APPENDIX VII

Drawing of Patent

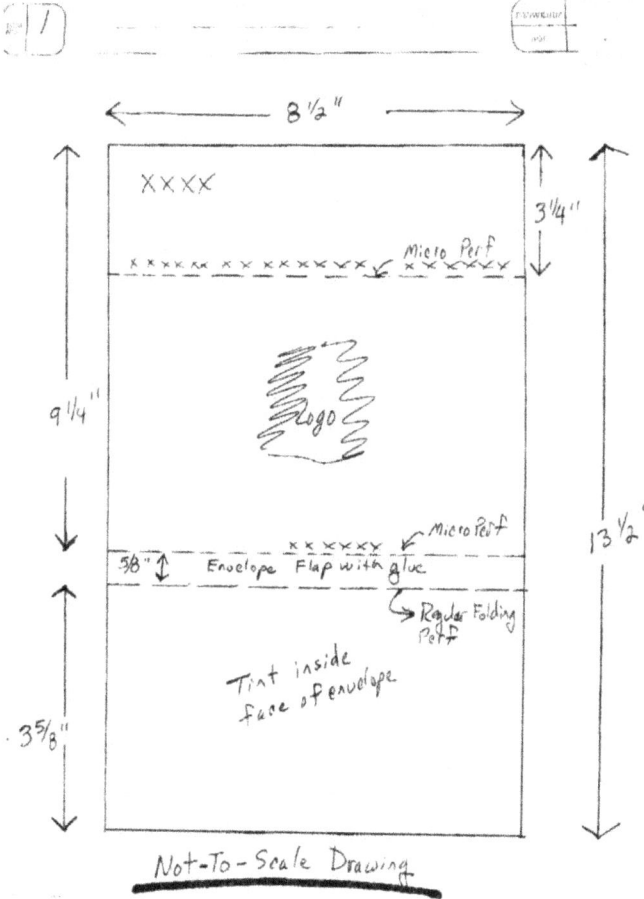

Not-To-Scale Drawing

www.ingramcontent.com/pod-product-compliance
Lightning Source LLC
Chambersburg PA
CBHW060616210326
41520CB00010B/1357